Women from North Move to South: Turkey's Female Movers from the Former Soviet Union Countries

TRANSNATIONAL PRESS LONDON

Books by TPL

Women from North Move to South: Turkey's Female Movers from the Former Soviet Union Countries

Turkish Migration Policy

Conflict, Insecurity, and Mobility

Family and Human Capital in Turkish Migration

Göç ve Uyum

Image of Istanbul: Impact of ECOC 2010 on the city image

Little Turkey in Great Britain

Overeducated and Over Here

Politics and Law in Turkish Migration

Turkish Migration, Identity and Integration

Journals by TPL

Migration Letters

Remittances Review

Göç Dergisi

Border Crossing

Journal of Gypsy Studies

Kurdish Studies

Transnational Marketing Journal

Women from North Move to South:

Turkey's Female Movers from the Former Soviet Union Countries

Oksana Koshulko

TRANSNATIONAL PRESS LONDON

2016

Women from North Move to South: Turkey's Female Movers from the Former Soviet Union Countries

by Oksana Koshulko

First Published in 2016 by TRANSNATIONAL PRESS LONDON in the United Kingdom, 12 Ridgeway Gardens, London, N6 5XR, UK.
www.tplondon.com

Paperback

ISBN: 978-1-910781-32-6

Cover Photo: Oksana Koshulko

Cover Design: Gizem Çakır

CONTENTS

TABLES

FIGURE

ACKNOWLEDGEMENTS

Firstly, I would like to express my sincere gratitude to my friend and proof-reader Judith Smith from the United Kingdom for her continuous support of my research, her patience, her moral support, her friendship, the motivation given to me, her continuous faith in me and her knowledge in areas of women's studies and gender. Her professionalism and positive support helped me throughout my research and the writing of this monograph. I could not have imagined having a better editor and proofreader for my monograph. It is thanks to the time and efforts of Judith Smith as proofreader and editor, that this monograph saw daylight.

My sincere thanks also go to my son Vladyslav Koshulko for his continuous support of my research and projects and his continuous faith in me. He has supported me spiritually both throughout the writing of this monograph and in my life in general.

I thank my colleagues Prof. Ibrahim Sirkeci from the Regent's University London, UK; Dr. Guncel Onkal from Maltepe University in Istanbul, Turkey; Prof. Dinara Peskova from the Bashkir Academy of Public Administration and Management under the President of Bashkortostan Republic; Prof. Zoran Cekerevac from the University "Union" - Nikola Tesla in Belgrade, Serbia for their help and continuous support of my international researches.

I also thank the Scientific & Technological Research Council of Turkey (TUBITAK) in Ankara, Maltepe University in Istanbul, and the organization 'Ukrainian Family' in Antalya, Turkey; the Network of East-West Women (NEWW), USA, and the Association for Women in Slavic Studies (AWSS), USA for their support for my research.

Last but not the least, I would like to thank my friends from Turkey and Ukraine, and my family, my parents and my brother for supporting me spiritually throughout the writing this monograph and in all aspects of my life.

ABOUT AUTHOR

Dr Oksana Koshulko earned her PhD in Economic Sciences at the National University of Food Technologies in Kyiv. She is an Associate Professor and a member of the Association for Women in Slavic Studies (AWSS), USA. Her scientific career includes international research experience funded by national and international scientific agencies in Poland, USA, Turkey and Canada. Dr Koshulko continues her international research career in areas of migration and women's studies, human capital and gender issues. Her papers have been published in international peer-reviewed journals and her books have been published in USA, Germany, Ukraine, Russia and England.

FOREWORD

Gender is still a relatively understudied topic in migration literature. Oksana Koshulko's study contributes to the field in this regard. It is also one of very few studies looking into migration to Turkey. Despite a recent rise in the number of studies focusing on immigrants in Turkey, particularly Syrian movers, the vast majority of the literature focuses on Turkish movers abroad.

Population movements between the Former Soviet Union countries and Turkey can date back to the 19th century, however, female movers, at least in a more visible fashion are rather a more recent phenomenon. The focus of the book is equally important given the prominent place of the former Soviet Union countries in Eurasian population movements. Former Soviet Union countries stand as one of the top immigration destinations in the world. This is a well-studied area in the Russian language but not much in the English language. Hence this is a timely and needed contribution. The study offers a comprehensive survey of Soviet nationalities from Tajiks to Tatars, Azeris, Armenians, and Uyghurs (Hereafter I will refer to them as "Soviet movers").

Koshulko's work offers rich material evidence to support the conflict model and culture of migration (see Sirkeci 2009; Cohen and Sirkeci, 2011; Sirkeci and Cohen, 2016). Movers from the selected countries were motivated by various discomforts, difficulties, tensions (i.e. conflicts) and yet they have faced an array of new hurdles in Turkey. This model suggests that migration is initiated by discomforts, tensions, conflicts of interest at the area of origin and new conflicts may arise during the process, which may lead to further movements (including remigration and return migration). Soviet movers in Koshulko's work are classified by their motives. Many from different nationalities arrived in Turkey for marriage. However, marriage is also a way to access the formal labour market in Turkey.

Koshulko's women show that marriages with Turkish men were often arranged in home countries. Since there are strong trade relations between these Former Soviet countries and Turkey, a sizeable volume of traffic exists. Many Turkish men visit these countries for short or long periods for work and business. We can argue that increased traffic, even in the form of tourism, contributes to the development of a culture of migration as these travels make both ends of the tourism routes familiar and turn them into potential destinations for migration. These trade and tourism relationships also serve as an opportunity framework for those who desire to move to another country.

International human mobility is driven by difficulties, unsatisfactory living and working conditions at home and more often than not directed towards countries where these difficulties and dissatisfaction can be seemingly addressed. Turkey, despite being placed at moderate level on Human Development Index scores table, compared to the countries of origin of Koshulko's Soviet movers, offers nominally higher average earnings. The desire to move is matched with relatively high income at destination.

Mixed motivations in human mobility are widely recognized now, both in academia and outside. Koshulko rightly draws the necessary parallels in political environment in the source countries and Turkey to show the disparity as a way of explaining the moves. Both relative political stability and less corruption in Turkey, compared to the countries of origin, and advantages of having Turkish citizenship were mentioned by Soviet movers who opted to settle in Turkey. At the same time, these women were seeking security and protection in Turkey and citizenship was thought to be instrumental in this respect. Of course, the networks, social and human capital and legal rules of admission might have all played a role in the decision of a destination.

Nevertheless, perception of paradise in the destination and troubles in the country of origin always fade a little in the face of new conflicts, difficulties, barriers, discomforts at the places of arrival. In many traditional destination countries, such as Germany, United Kingdom and France, one form of these conflicts is manifested as racism and discrimination. Nevertheless, there are subtler issues such as not knowing the culture surrounding the way in which business is done and relationships are established, as well as practical barriers such as speaking the language of the destination. Koshulko's analysis of the destination begins with the language barrier.

Language is a decisive component in migration decision making. It is a part of human capital which plays a key role in choosing the destination. However, people do not always go to places where they can speak the language. Understandably those coming from countries where Turkic languages are spoken have an advantage in learning the Turkish language.

Although, in Turkish discourse, tolerance and hospitality are frequently key words, a significant number of Soviet movers, including those with Turkic origins, have experienced discrimination in Turkey; some also experienced discrimination within the families of their Turkish husbands. Domestic violence and abuse is also mentioned as the most common of issues. These all fall under relative human insecurity in our

Conflict Model (Sirkeci, 2009) and are likely to be triggers for further migrations.

Relative insecurity also emerges in the form of occupational mismatches. In the United Kingdom, based on years of analysis, we have found that particularly visible minorities such as Blacks and Muslims, as well as Eastern Europeans, face labour market disadvantages and discrimination (Sirkeci et al., 2014; Saunders, 2015). Unsurprisingly, the issue is not unique to Western Europe or North America. Over 80 percent of Soviet movers in Turkey, Koshulko reports in her fifth chapter were doing jobs other than their profession. This study also provides evidence for insecurity in terms of domestic violence and gender inequalities, which put women in a difficult place.

It is highly recommended that to comprehend migration processes, one should take a holistic view where countries of origin, destination, and transit are important but also movement is conceptualized as an open ended process which is responsive to conflicts which are likely to evolve, emerge, and fade away over time and space. Koshulko's attempt to capture problems faced by returnee Soviet movers back in their countries of origin after a spell in Turkey is, therefore, valuable.

The cultures of migration are built over time and established with movement. As we discussed prominently elsewhere, households and families play a crucial role in the migration process. Migration is hard and is rarely a decision made in isolation by individuals. Similarly, repercussions of migration affect a wider network of people. This wider impact is where we also underline the role and involvement of non-movers in decisions to move.

Koshulko's children left behind are part of these non-movers related to Soviet mothers in Turkey. Some others are simply dependent children moved with their mothers. Some are yet unborn but their mothers' mobility experience will have a bearing on their life choices and trajectories.

Despite the turmoil that unfolded in Turkey after the failed coup attempt on 15th July 2016, the traffic between Turkey and her neighbours to the north is unlikely to stop. It may temporarily slow down but already established migration routes, personal and business networks, as well as the experience of population movements over the years, are the guarantees for this culture of migration to survive.

This book is a pioneering study of female movers from the Former Soviet Union countries and raises a number of questions which, hopefully, will be taken up by other researchers to expand the knowledge in this specific stream of migration or one may also call it "Soviet-Turkish culture of migration". There is more work to be done to understand this particular migratory regime but a start is always good news.

Professor Ibrahim Sirkeci

Regent's Centre for Transnational Studies

Regent's University London, United Kingdom

INTRODUCTION

In this book, I have explored the struggles they face and the lives of migrant women who moved from the countries of the former Soviet Union to Turkey. Understanding migrant women and their experiences is important as an understudied aspect of human mobility.

Women from all countries of the Former Soviet Union, who live, work or study in Turkey have been covered in this book. The majority of women whose experiences I talk about were married to Turkish men and were living mainly in Istanbul, Izmir, Antalya and Ankara for large cities in Turkey.

About 400 women reached by snowball sampling were interviewed and the results are presented and discussed in this book. Also a few men who were married to migrant women were interviewed while wider context was established by taking opinions of lawyers and researchers in this field of research.

This book consists of a preface, the introduction, eight chapters, the conclusions, the bibliography and the acknowledgements. The characteristics of female migrants in Turkey from the countries of the Former Soviet Union, their nationalities, citizenships and religions are explored in this chapter; the classification of groups of female migrants from the countries of the Former Soviet Union, in Turkey are presented in chapter one; the characteristics of the socio-economic and political situation in the countries of the Former Soviet Union and Turkey to frame the movement of women from the former to the latter are covered in chapter two, so explaining the circumstances trigerring migration to Turkey ; Common problems of female migrants from the Former Soviet Union countries in Turkey are explored in chapter three, while the remaining chapters focus on human capital aspects, common patterns and characteristics of movers, and the support available for these movers in Turkey.

This book is important as a detailed preliminary examination of experiences of migrant women from Former Soviet Union countries in Turkey but also as a contribution to gender studies and international relations. In the book, sometimes I have used the term "Soviet women" as a shorthand to refer to female migrants who moved from the former Soviet Union countries to Turkey.

Who are the women who moved from the former Soviet countries to Turkey?

From September 2014 to June 2015, I interviewed hundreds of migrant women of different ethnic groups and nationalities from Armenia, Azerbaijan, Belarus, Estonia, Georgia, Kazakhstan, Kyrgyzstan, Latvia, Lithuania, Moldova, Russia, Tajikistan, Turkmenistan, Ukraine, and Uzbekistan (Table 0.1).

Table 0.1. Nationalities and ethnic groups of women from the countries of the Former Soviet Union, participants of the project

Countries	Nationalities	Ethnic groups
Armenia	The Armenians	Armenian
Azerbaijan	The Azerbaijanis	Turkic
	The Russians	East Slavic
Belarus	The Belarusians	East Slavic
Estonia	The Estonians	Finnic
Georgia	The Georgians	Georgian
	The Abkhazians	Caucasian
Kazakhstan	The Kazakhs	Turkic
	The Uyghurs	Turkic
Kyrgyzstan	The Kyrghyz	Turkic
	The Uyghurs	Turkic
Latvia	The Latvians	Baltic
Lithuania	The Lithuanians	Baltic
Moldova	The Moldovans	Moldovan
	The Gagauz	Turkic population
	The Romanians	Romanian
Russia	The Russians	East Slavic
	The Buryat	Buryat
	The Yakuts	Turkic people
	The Lezgins	Lezgic
	The Tatars	Turkic people
	The Kabardians	Adyghe
Tajikistan	The Russians	East Slavic
Turkmenistan	The Turkmens	Turkic people
	The Laks	Lak
	The Iranians	Iranic peoples
Ukraine	The Ukrainians	East Slavic
	The Poles	West Slavic
	The Crimean Tatars	Turkic
Uzbekistan	The Uzbeks	Turkic
	The Tatars	Turkic people

In my project Armenia was represented by one nationality, the Armenians. Azerbaijan was represented by two nationalities, the Azerbaijanis and the Russians. Belarus was represented by one nationality, the Belarusians. Georgia was represented by two nationalities, the Georgians and the Abkhazians. Kazakhstan was represented by two nationalities, Kazakhs and the Uyghurs. Kyrgyzstan was represented by two nationalities, the Kyrghyz and the Uyghurs. Estonia, Latvia, and Lithuania were represented by three nationalities, the Estonians; the Latvians; and the Lithuanians. Moldova was represented by three nationalities, the Moldovans, the Gagauz, and the Romanians. Russia was represented by several nationalities and ethnic groups including the Russians, the Buryats, the Yakuts of the Sakha Republic, the Lezgic, the Tatars, and the Kabardians. Tajikistan was represented by one nationality, the Russians, not the Tajiks. Turkmenistan was represented by three nationalities, the Turkmens, the Laks, and the Iranians. Ukraine was represented by three nationalities, the Ukrainians, the Crimean Tatars, and the Poles. Uzbekistan was represented by two nationalities, the Tatars and the Uzbeks.

For other ethnic groups the process of adaptation and integration in the host country is more difficult. Table 0.2 presents the characteristics of different ethnic groups, Turkic and others, who currently live in Turkey.

Some of these ethnic groups and nationalities are Turkic groups, and for women of Turkic ethnic groups it is much easier and faster to adapt and integrate in Turkey. These ethnic groups are Azerbaijanis, Kazakhs, Kyrghyz, Gagauz, Yakuts, Uyghurs, Tatars, Crimean Tatars, Turkmens, and Uzbeks.

Those belonging to the Turkic ethnic group:

The Azerbaijanis are a Turkic ethnic group and live on the four continents of the world in many countries including Turkey. There are studies on issues of Azeri Women in Soviet and Post-Soviet Azerbaijan (Heyat 2002) and on problems and difficulties faced by Azerbaijani women in Antalya, Turkey (Ozgur et al., 2014).

The Kazakhs are a Turkic ethnic group and live in Central Asia and some countries of Europe, as Laruelle explored the new migration crossroads in Kazakhstan (Laruelle 2013). The Kyrgyz are also a Turkic ethnic group and the majority of them live in Central Asia and their migration has been analysed (Agadjanian and Agadjanian, 2010).

The Gagauz are a Turkic population. The Uyghurs are a Turkic ethnic group who live in Eastern and Central Asia. The Tatars are Turkic people who live in Asia and Europe. The Crimean Tatars are a Turkic ethnic group who came back to the Crimean Peninsula after deportation in 1944. The Turkmens are a Turkic people who are located in Central Asia. The Uzbeks are the largest Turkic ethnic group in Central Asia. The Yakuts also belong to the Turkic people.

Table 0.2. Showing the Turkic, Slavic and other ethnic groups and populations, which include women, who participated in structured interviews in the framework of the scientific project

Representatives of ethnic groups	A Turkic ethnic group	Representatives of ethnic groups	Other ethnic groups
The Azerbaijanis	A Turkic	The Armenians	Armenian
The Kazakhs	A Turkic	The Ukrainians	East Slavic
The Kyrghyz	A Turkic	The Belarusians	East Slavic
The Gagauz	A Turkic population	The Russians	East Slavic
The Yakuts	Turkic people	The Poles	West Slavic
The Uyghurs	A Turkic	The Abkhazians	Caucasian
The Tatars	Turkic people	The Latvians	Baltic
The Crimean Tatars	A Turkic	The Lithuanians	Baltic
The Turkmens	Turkic people	The Estonians	Finnic
The Uzbeks	A Turkic	The Moldovans	Moldovan
		The Romanians	Romanian
		The Buryat	Buryat
		The Georgians	Georgian
		The Lezgins	Lezgic
		The Laks	Lak
		The Iranians	Iranic peoples
		The Kabardians	Adyghe

The Armenians are an ethnic group who live in numerous countries of North and South America, Europe, and Asia including Turkey (Voss-Wittig 2007).

The Ukrainians, the Belarusians and the Russians are East Slavic ethnic groups currently living in North and South America, Europe and Asia. In recent decades numerous Ukrainian, Belarusian and Russian women have married Turkish citizens.

Mary Zirin and colleagues have studied women from Central and Eastern Europe, Russia and Eurasia in their book, including Ukrainian, Belarusian, and Russian women (Zirin et al., 2007).

The Poles are a nation and a West Slavic ethnic group. The Romanians are a Romanian ethnic group. The Moldovans are a Moldovan ethnic group and a subgroup of the Romanian ethnic group and were investigated by Unal regarding their work as domestic workers (Unal, 2008). The Georgians are a nation and ethnic group who live in North America, Europe and Asia including Turkey and their identity, religion, and modernity in the Republic of Georgia were explored earlier (Pelkmans, 2006).

The Abkhazians (see Hewitt, 2015) are a Caucasian ethnic group, who live in Europe and Asia and a large Diaspora arrived in Turkey.

The Latvians and the Lithuanians are Baltic ethnic groups who live in North and South America, Australia, and Eurasia. The Estonians are a Finnic ethnic group. Joseph Suad and Afsana Nagmabadi have explored women of these ethnic groups in their book "Encyclopedia of Women and Islamic Cultures: Family, Law and Politics" (Suad, 2003).

The Buryat are a Buryat ethnic group and a subgroup of the Mongols. The Lezgins are a Lezgic ethnic group who live in Azerbaijan and Dagestan. The Laks are an indigenous people of the Caucasus and are the fifth largest ethnic group in Dagestan. The Iranians are Iranic peoples who live in Iran and outside of Iran including Turkmenistan. The Kabardians are an Adyghe (Circassian) ethnic group.

So, participants in this research were women of different nationalities and ethnic groups from 15 countries of the Former USSR who live in Turkey, representing 27 nationalities and ethnic groups. Ten or 37% of these nationalities and ethnic groups are Turkic people. Female migrants from these Turkic groups may adapt in the host country more easily than women of other nationalities and ethnic groups who moved to Turkey.

Citizenship among the female movers from the Former Soviet Union

As noted above, women from countries of the Former Soviet Union are of different nationalities and women with the same nationality can have different citizenships from within countries of the Former Soviet Union.

Table 0.3 displays nationalities and citizenships of women from countries of the Former Soviet Union who were resident in Turkey at the time of the research. Women who moved from Armenia had Turkish citizenship (33%); Armenian citizenship (44%), and Russian citizenship (23%). Female movers from Azerbaijan had Turkish citizenship (42%); Azerbaijani citizenship (54%), and Russian citizenship (4%). Female movers from Belarus had Turkish citizenship (29%); Moldavian (3%) Belarusian (65%), and Lithuanian citizenship (3%).

Table 0.3. Nationalities and citizenship among female movers from the countries of the Former Soviet Union resident in Turkey

Citizenships	%	Citizenships	%	Citizenships	%
Nationalities					
Armenians					
Turkish	33	Russian	23	Armenian	44
Azerbaijanis					
Turkish	42	Russian	4	Azerbaijani	54
Belarusians					
Turkish	29	Belarusian	65	Moldavian	3
Lithuanian	3				
Estonians					
Estonian	100				
Georgians					
Turkish	18	Georgian	73	Russian	9
Kazakhs					
Turkish	32	Kyrgyz	5	Ukrainian	5
Turkmen	5	Kazakhstani	53		
Kyrghyz					
Turkish	27	Kyrgyz	73		
Latvians					
Turkish	20	Latvian	80		
Lithuanians					
Lithuanian	100				
Moldovans					
Turkish	38	Moldovan	52	Ukrainian	3
Bulgarian	7				
Russians					
Turkish	31	Ukrainian	7	Russian	54
Other	8				
Russians					
Tajik	100				
Turkmens					
Turkish	15	Turkmen	85		
Ukrainians					
Turkish	25	Ukrainian	73	Other	2
Uzbeks					
Turkish	36	Russian	9	Uzbek	46
Kyrgyz	9				

All female movers from Estonia were Estonian citizens. Women from Georgia had Turkish citizenship (18%); Georgian citizenship (73%), and Russian citizenship (9%). Women from Kazakhstan had Turkish citizenship (32%); Ukrainian citizenship (5%), Kazakhstani citizenship (53%), Kyrgyz citizenship (5%), and Turkmen citizenship (5%). Female movers from Kyrgyzstan had Turkish citizenship (27%); and Kyrgyz citizenship (73%). Women from Latvia had Turkish (20%) and Latvian (80%) citizenships, while all female movers from Lithuania were Lithuanian citizens.

Moldovan women had Turkish citizenship (38%), Ukrainian citizenship (3%), Moldovan citizenship (52%) and Bulgarian citizenship (7%). Russian women had Turkish citizenship (30%), Russian citizenship (55%), Ukrainian citizenship (7%) and citizenship of other countries (8%). Turkmen women had Turkish citizenship (15%), and Turkmen citizenship (85%). Ukrainian women had Turkish citizenship (25%), Ukrainian citizenship (73%) and citizenship of other countries (2%). Uzbek women had Turkish citizenship (36%), Uzbek citizenship (46%), Russian citizenship (9%) and Kyrgyz citizenship (9%).

As noted above, a large portion of women from the countries of the Former USSR obtained dual citizenship in Turkey (International Labor Organization, 2009). However the majority of countries of the Former USSR do not allow their citizens to have dual citizenships. According to the United States Department of State (DOS), "The concept of dual nationality means that a person is a national of two countries at the same time. Each country has its own nationality laws based on its own policy. Persons may have dual nationality by automatic operation of different laws rather than by choice" (United States Department of State 2016). So, the majority of the countries of the former USSR do not allow their own citizens to have dual citizenship, and among these are Azerbaijan, Belarus, Estonia, Georgia, Kazakhstan, Lithuania, Tajikistan, Turkmenistan, Ukraine, Uzbekistan, and others. Some countries allow dual citizenships including Armenia and Latvia. Of course, advantages and disadvantages exist for those having dual citizenships, and for women from the countries of the Former USSR these advantages are feelings of security and stability during their time in the host country.

Religion among women from the countries of the Former Soviet Union resident in Turkey

During field research, I met women of different religions including Christianity (including Jehovah's Witnesses); Islam; Agnosticism; Buddhism; and Atheist (Table 0.4).

These are the dominant religions in the countries of the former USSR in reference to the full classification of most popular World Religions and Sects by Richard Grigonis (Grigonis, 2014). So, the largest and dominant religion in Turkey is Islam. Among the countries of the Former

Soviet Union Islam is the most important religion in Azerbaijan, Kazakhstan, Kyrgyzstan, Tajikistan, Turkmenistan, and Uzbekistan.

Table 0.4. Religions among female movers from the Former Soviet Union in Turkey

Countries of the Former Soviet Union	The most important religions of these countries
Armenia	Christianity
Azerbaijan	Islam
Belarus	Eastern Orthodox
Estonia	Orthodox and Lutheran Christianity
Georgia	Orthodox Christianity
Kazakhstan	Islam
Kyrgyzstan	Islam
Latvia	Christianity
Lithuania	Christianity
Moldova	Christianity
Russia	Russian Orthodox
Tajikistan	Islam
Turkmenistan	Islam
Ukraine	Roman Catholic and Eastern Orthodox
Uzbekistan	Islam

The most important religion of Armenia is Christianity; of Belarus it is Eastern Orthodox; of Estonia it is Orthodox and Lutheran Christianity; of Georgia it is Orthodox Christianity; of Latvia, Lithuania, and Moldova it is Christianity; of Russia it is Russian Orthodox; and of Ukraine it is Roman Catholic and Eastern Orthodox.

Women from Azerbaijan, Kazakhstan, Kyrgyzstan, Turkmenistan and Uzbekistan have the same religion as Turkey, and so they feel more comfortable in Turkish society than women from Armenia, Belarus, Estonia, Georgia, Latvia, Lithuania, Moldova, Russia, and Ukraine. Some of the women of non-Muslim countries of the Former USSR convert to Islam for a variety of reasons.

There are also Christian women from Muslim and non-Muslim countries of the Former Soviet Union who convert to Islam for various reasons after arrival in Turkey. The main reason for converting to Islam is the desire of Christian women to marry Turkish men. Christian women who would like to marry Turkish men have often felt (or were sometimes required) that they should convert to Islam.

"Sookhdeo (Sookhdeo, 2007) believes that some 30,000 Westerners have converted to Islam in the last decade - the majority of them women. Clearly, our churches need to do something about this. In Sunday school classes and youth groups, we need to teach our childresn, especially our daughters, about the difference between Islam and Christianity. And we cannot forget the role that Christian education plays here. We must remind them of the Apostle Paul's admonition in Second Corinthians that we not be yoked with unbelievers" (The Christian Broadcasting Network 2016).

According to Surat Al-Baqarah [verse 221] of the Quran, a Holy Book of Muslims about their way of life and obedience to Allah, it is possible to find an answer to the question about marriage of a Muslim man and a Christian woman:

Surah Al-Baqarah [2:221] - Al-Qur'an al-Kareem "And do not marry polytheistic women until they believe. And a believing slave woman is better than a polytheist, even though she might please you. And do not marry polytheistic men [to your women] until they believe. And a believing slave is better than a polytheist, even though he might please you. Those invite [you] to the Fire, but Allah invites to Paradise and to forgiveness, by His permission. And He makes clear His verses to the people that perhaps they may remember" (Quran).

Therefore, one of the reasons why Christian women from the countries of the Former Soviet Union have converted to Islam is marriage to Muslim men in Turkey, primarily of Turkish and Kurdish nationalities.

Among the participants of this current research, 8 to 22% of Christian women from Muslim and non-Muslim countries of the Former Soviet Union have converted to Islam. Table 0.5 showing the percentage of women who have converted to Islam in various countries.

According to responses of Christian women from Muslim and non-Muslim countries of the Former Soviet Union within this scientific project, 8 to 22% of them have converted to Islam, 8% of Christian women from Kazakhstan and Russia; 9% of Christian women from Kyrgyzstan; 14% of women from Ukraine; 15% of women from Moldova; and 22% of women from Georgia.

During my research I met women who have converted to Islam, but I also met women who have converted to Islam and then become as apostates because a decision to convert to Islam is a very serious and difficult decision, and with time some Christian women understood that their decision to convert to Islam was a mistake.

I also met Christian women in Turkey, who have remained convinced of their faith and have not changed their religion even for marriage to Muslim men in Turkey.

Table 0.5. Percentage of Christian women who have converted to Islam

Muslim and non-Muslim countries of the Former Soviet Union	The percentage of Christian women who have converted to Islam, in %
Georgia	22
Kazakhstan	8
Kyrgyzstan	9
Moldova	15
Russia	8
Ukraine	14

There are also women who have converted to Islam and have found in Islam their true religion. The decision to convert to Islam is a very personal choice, and not everyone can do it. Other reasons why women can convert to Islam are:

-the desire to receive generous gifts and / or gold from Turkish husbands and their relatives due to conversion to Islam;

-the desire to feel themselves more comfortable with Turkish husbands among Muslim families in Muslim society;

-the desire to have a faith, if they did not have faith when they were Christians.

Muslim men differ from each other in their degree of faith, or religiousness. If Muslim men, husbands of women from the Former Soviet Union countries, are very religious, they may force their wives to wear the clothes and coverings of Muslim women. The BBC presented a classification of different kinds of coverings worn by Muslim women (BBC 2015):

⊃ "the word **hijab** describes the act of covering up generally but is often used to describe the headscarves worn by Muslim women;

⊃ The **niqab** is a veil for the face that leaves the area around the eyes clear. However, it may be worn with a separate eye veil. It is worn with an accompanying headscarf;

⊃ The **burka** is the most concealing of all Islamic veils. It is a one-piece veil that covers the face and body, often leaving just a mesh screen to see through;

⊃   The **al-amira** is a two-piece veil. It consists of a close fitting cap, usually made from cotton or polyester, and a tube-like scarf;

⊃   The **shayla** is a long, rectangular scarf. It is wrapped around the head and tucked or pinned in place at the shoulders;

⊃   The **khimar** is a long, cape-like veil that hangs down to just above the waist. It covers the hair, neck and shoulders completely, but leaves the face clear;

⊃   The **chador** is a full-body cloak. It is often accompanied by a smaller headscarf underneath" (BBC 2015).

However, the first President of Turkey Mustafa Kemal Ataturk (1881-1938), the reformer of Turkey, allowed the freedom to wear modern clothing: "Abolishment of carsaf and veil, allowing women to have the freedom to wear modern clothing" (Sumer 2013).

If Muslim men, husbands of women from the Former Soviet Union countries are less religious, their wives do not wear clothes and coverings of Muslim women, but they need to follow Turkish traditions and holidays such as a holy month of fasting and prayers named Ramadan, and others holidays.

Surah Al-Baqarah [2:183-185] - Al-Qur'an al-Kareem: "O you who have believed, decreed upon you is fasting as it was decreed upon those before you that you may become righteous"; "The month of Ramadhan [is that] in which was revealed the Qur'an, a guidance for the people and clear proofs of guidance and criterion. So whoever sights [the new moon of] the month, let him fast it; and whoever is ill or on a journey - then an equal number of other days. Allah intends for you ease and does not intend for your hardship and [wants] for you to complete the period and to glorify Allah for that [to] which He has guided you; and perhaps you will be grateful" (Quran).

Hence I conclude that these women make their own choice with or without pressure from their Muslim relatives and they need to take into account the consequences of their conversion to Islam.

These consequences may include:

⊃   To become an apostate with time;

⊃   not to be accepted as a Muslim member of a family and not to be accepted as a Christian member of a family in the country of origin;

⊃ To lead a double life, meaning to show commitment to Islamic traditions, clothes and culture, but not to truly believe.

⊃ But worst consequences may be when a woman decides to become an apostate sometime later. In these cases, a woman can face domestic violence and abuse, and psychological problems.

Unfortunately, domestic violence and abuse is not a rare occurrence in the existing families. In this study it was found that domestic violence and abuse were reported by 14% of the Azerbaijani women; 8% of the Belarusian and the Kazakhstan women; 35% of the Moldovan women; 9% of the Russian and the Turkmen women; 17% of the Ukrainian women, and 71% of the Uzbek women.

Reasons for Muslim men to marry women from the countries of the Former Soviet Union

The current residence of women from territories of countries of the Former Soviet Union in Turkey is not a modern phenomenon. Such women have been living in Turkey for many centuries, since the reign of Roxelana (Hurrem Sultan) or even earlier. According to data from Susan Ozmore in her article "The Sultanate of Women" (Ozmore 2013):

Hurrem Sultan (c. 1500-1558) was born Alexandra Anastasia Lisowska, or Roxelana, in the town of Rohatyn in what was then the Kingdom of Poland and is now in western Ukraine. The area was often subject to raiding by Crimean Tatars, and during one raid Roxelana was taken captive and sold as a slave. Taken to Istanbul, she was selected for Suleiman's harem. After a time, she became his actual legal wife. This was rare and gave Hurrem great influence (Ozmore 2013).

Women from the territories of the countries of the Former Soviet Union, especially from Slavic countries, historically were attractive to Muslim men. According to Gabriel Sawma a lawyer with a Middle Eastern background (Sawma 2013):

"Early Muslim jurists ruled that the marriage of a Muslim man to a Christian or Jewish woman is considered "makruh" (not desirable) if both live in a non-Muslim country. In fact, the second Caliph, Umar bin Al-Khattab (634-644), denied interfaith marriage for Muslim men during his term as "Amir al-Muminin" (Prince of the Believers, i.e. Muslims).

However, the majority of Muslim jurists in modern days do not prohibit a Muslim man from marrying a Christian or Jewish woman; this, in their view, ensures that over many centuries, the Islamic patriarchal society would gain more adherents to Islam relative to Christianity, Judaism and other co-existing religions. Additionally, a

Christian or Jewish wife will face difficulty converting Muslim husband into their religion.

Table 0.6 - Gender in Turkey's population, age group (15-64), 1935-2015

Year	Total	Male	Female	Proportion (%)		
				M	F	T
1935	8 795 512	4 130 788	4 664 724	47,0	53,0	100
1940	9 668 796	4 626 079	5 042 717	47,8	52,2	100
1945	10 717 968	5 258 500	5 459 468	49,1	50,9	100
1950	12 211 300	6 046 994	6 164 306	49,5	50,5	100
1955	13 729 233	6 942 990	6 786 243	50,6	49,4	100
1960	15 299 311	7 806 612	7 492 699	51,0	49,0	100
1965	16 953 850	8 612 026	8 341 824	50,8	49,2	100
1970	19 152 564	9 660 942	9 491 622	50,4	49,6	100
1975	22 086 237	11 364 541	10 721 696	51,5	48,5	100
1980	25 022 358	12 670 034	12 352 324	50,6	49,4	100
1985	29 432 295	14 881 386	14 550 909	50,6	49,4	100
1990	34 265 838	17 334 960	16 930 878	50,6	49,4	100
2000	43 701 502	22 131 543	21 569 959	50,6	49,4	100
2007	46 943 690	23 655 657	23 288 033	50,4	49,6	100
2008	47 835 090	24 114 713	23 720 377	50,4	49,6	100
2009	48 618 564	24 557 794	24 060 770	50,5	49,5	100
2010	49 516 670	25 020 856	24 495 814	50,5	49,5	100
2011	50 346 979	25 440 290	24 906 689	50,5	49,5	100
2012	51 088 202	25 803 873	25 284 329	50,5	49,5	100
2013	51 926 356	26 237 038	25 689 318	50,5	49,5	100
2014	52 640 512	26 601 724	26 038 788	50,5	49,5	100
2015	53 359 594	26 972 558	26 387 036	50,5	49,5	100

Source: TurkStat

The following are the legal impacts of a Muslim man marrying Christian or Jewish wife: -a Muslim man's ability to have more thanone wife at a time; -children born of such marriages are considered Muslims; -in the event of divorce, or death of the husband, Islamic Sharia determines that in mixed marriages where the husband is Muslim and the wife is not, the wife will lose custody of the children; -wife cannot travel with her children without the permission of the husband; -a husband traveling with the children to an Islamic country may decide to stay in his home country; -conversion of one spouse to Islam; -inheritance. The general rule in Islamic Sharia is that women inherit half the share of men who have the same degree of relation to the deceased; Muslim women are prohibited from marrying non-Muslim Mmn" (Sawma 2013). Thus, according to Islamic Sharia rules, Muslim men seem to have total control over their non-Muslim wives and this is the first and the main reason why the men would like to marry Christian women from the countries of the Former Soviet Union.

The second reason why Turkish men would like to marry women from the countries of the Former Soviet Union can be the fact that there are fewer women than men Turkey (Table 0.6).

According to data of the Turkish Statistical Institute, the number of male population prevails over female population in Turkey. Thus, a percentage of the male population of Turkey in age 15-64 years in 1935 was 47%; in 1940 was 48%; in 1945 was 49%; in 1950 was 49.5%; and since this period the male population of Turkey has increased. The number of males in Turkey's population has changed signiciantly from 1955, when it was 50.5%; and changed to 51% in 1960, 50.4% in 1970; 50.6 in 1980 to 50.6 in 2000; 50.4 in 2007; 50.5% in 2010; and 50.55% in 2015 (Turkish Statistical Institute 2016). Since 1950, the male population of Turkey of age 15-64 increased and is larger than the female population (Table 0.7).

Therefore, the difference between female and male population of Turkey aged 15-64 in 1955 was 156747, but 60 years later, in 2015, this difference was already 585522 or more than half of million. This might be reason for Turkish men to marry women from the former USSR countries.

The third reason why Muslim men would like to marry women from the countries of the Former Soviet Union is their beauty and high level of education. I had an interview with an architect from Istanbul for example. He was married to a Ukrainian woman, and he told me that he values this woman because she was a beautiful, smart, clever, intelligent and educated woman.

Female migrants of different nationalities, citizenships and religions from the countries of the Former Soviet Union come to Turkey and each one of them finds themselves a place here. Some women from the Former USSR were of Turkic ethnic origin, and, these women seem to feel very much at home in Turkey because they share the same religion and speak a Turkic language. Hence they can adapt in the host country quickly and easily.

Other women from non-Muslim countries of the Former USSR belonging to other ethnic and linguistic groups face difficulties in the host country. Some of them have converted to Islam. Women from the countries of the Former USSR who are Christians, according to Surat Al-Baqarah [verse 221] of the Quran, a Holy Book of Muslims, may marry Muslim men when they convert to Islam. In this study, Christian female respondents from Muslim and non-Muslim countries of the Former Soviet Union have converted to Islam, 8 to 22% depending on nationality: 8% of Christian women from Kazakhstan and Russia; 9% of

Christian women from Kyrgyzstan; 14% of women from Ukraine; 15% of women from Moldova; and 22% of women from Georgia.

Table 0.7. The difference in number of male and female populations of Turkey aged 15-64, 1935-2015

Year	Total	Male	Female	The difference
1935	8 795 512	4 130 788	4 664 724	-533 936
1940	9 668 796	4 626 079	5 042 717	-416 638
1945	10 717 968	5 258 500	5 459 468	-200 968
1950	12 211 300	6 046 994	6 164 306	-117 312
1955	13 729 233	6 942 990	6 786 243	156 747
1960	15 299 311	7 806 612	7 492 699	313 913
1965	16 953 850	8 612 026	8 341 824	270 202
1970	19 152 564	9 660 942	9 491 622	169 320
1975	22 086 237	11 364 541	10 721 696	642 845
1980	25 022 358	12 670 034	12 352 324	317 710
1985	29 432 295	14 881 386	14 550 909	330 477
1990	34 265 838	17 334 960	16 930 878	404 082
2000	43 701 502	22 131 543	21 569 959	561 584
2007	46 943 690	23 655 657	23 288 033	367 624
2008	47 835 090	24 114 713	23 720 377	394 336
2009	48 618 564	24 557 794	24 060 770	497 024
2010	49 516 670	25 020 856	24 495 814	525 042
2011	50 346 979	25 440 290	24 906 689	533 601
2012	51 088 202	25 803 873	25 284 329	519 544
2013	51 926 356	26 237 038	25 689 318	547 720
2014	52 640 512	26 601 724	26 038 788	562 936
2015	53 359 594	26 972 558	26 387 036	585 522

In brief, reasons for Muslim men to marry women from the countries of the Former USSR include their desire to have total control over these women because the rules in Islamic Sharia allow Muslim men to have total control over their non-Muslim wives; the number of women in Turkey is less than that of men; and women from the countries of the Former Soviet Union are beautiful, capable, and educated to a high level.

CHAPTER 1

MOTIVATIONS, SATISFACTION, EXPECTATIONS AND CAREERS IN TURKEY

I have looked at the experiences of female migrants from the countries of the Former Soviet Union from different angles (i.e. classifications) to understand them better (Koshulko, 2016). Women have their own reasons for coming to Turkey - to study, to work, to start and develop a business, or to marry. Thus, the first classification relates to the reasons why the women arrived in the host country:

- ⊃ The first reason why female migrants arrive in the host country is in order to achieve professional goals. This category constitutes a small percentage of all women from the countries of the Former Soviet Union because is not easy for women to find a legal job with a contract of employment;

- ⊃ The second reason why female migrants arrive in the host country is for business because some business women are already owners of companies and are also employers. The majority of these businesses are in tourism, the service sector or commerce in Turkey;

- ⊃ The third reason why women arrive is labor migration. Labor migrants work in the host country legally or illegally;

- ⊃ The fourth reason why women arrive is for illegal activity and because of this some of them find that they become victims of Human Trafficking;

- ⊃ The fifth reason why women arrive is to take seasonal jobs in the hotels of the Turkish tourist trade;

- ⊃ The sixth reason why women arrive from the countries of the Former Soviet Union is to pursue educational careers in schools or universities in Turkey.

- ⊃ The last, seventh, reason why female migrants come is for marriage to Turkish citizens. These women from the countries of the Former Soviet Union come en masse to marry in Turkey.

If women have lived a normal fulfilling life in their countries of origin, the majority of them would like to continue this style of life after marriage in Turkey. However, very often these women face numerous restrictions in their new families and from their husbands' relatives. If they cannot accept this situation, it can lead to domestic violence, abuse and /or divorce.

The second classification relates to the degree of access to a normal fulfilling life for women from the countries of the Former Soviet Union in families and in society and depends upon the educational level and the religion of their husbands and his relatives.

The first degree of access to a normal fulfilling life for women is 'visible' women, who live a normal fulfilling life and can work in the host country because their husbands understand all the difficulties their wives face in adapting and integrating into Turkish society;

The second degree of access to a normal fulfilling life for women is "invisible" women who live with the numerous restrictions in families in the host society. Very often these women have converted to Islam and cannot work because their husbands do not accede to the wishes of their wives and these women live according to rules laid down by their husbands and relatives of husbands;

The third degree of access to a normal fulfilling life of women is 'semi-invisible' women who live with the numerous restrictions in families in the host country but in their countries of origin during their vacations or holidays they can continue a normal fulfilling life as they did before their marriage. These women lead double lives.

Sometimes the woman's desire to marry aTurkish man stems from the 'Eastern fairy tale', when women dream about 'princes', and they think that their lives will be wonderful in the host country after marriage (Ashman & Gokmen, 2006).

Many women have high expectations that a "social elevator," brought about by marriage, will change their lives for the better in the host country.

Pitirim Sorokin in his book "Social mobility" has explained that "social elevator" refers to moving from the very bottom of a society to the top (Sorokin, 1998).

The third classification relates to the expectations of women of a "social elevator" resulting from marriage in Turkey:

The first category of women does receive a better quality of life due to marriage but the percentage of these women is small compared with all women from the countries of the Former Soviet Union who marry in Turkey;

The second category of women had high expectations of improving their standard of living and quality of life in Turkey and they try to find a way of improving their and their future children's lives through marriage. However, their expectations are not realized and some of them return to their country of origin after divorce and someone try to stay in Turkey to find another relationship. This "social elevator" concept was studied by Jovanovic (Jovanovic 2007).

The next classification relates to the building of careers by female immigrants in Turkey. If these women are Muslim, for example from Azerbaijan or Turkmenistan, the majority of them will not try to build a career in the host country because marriage and children are the main occupation in their lives. However, women from Ukraine, Belarus, Russia and other countries of the Former USSR will try to build their career. So, the fourth classification relates to the building of careers by female immigrants in the host country.

Some women come to Turkey to marry and do not want to build any career there. Their main intention is to have a family and children.

Women who thought the same as those in the first category but later on feel the necessity to seek self-fulfilment as professionals in the host country.

Women for whom continuation of their career was the most important thing and who confirm their diplomas in Turkey or seek out additional education there in order to get employment in different international organizations and companies. Very often these groups of women are divorcées.

Reasons why women from the countries of the Former Soviet Union move to Turkey.

I conducted structured interviews among women from the countries of the Former Soviet Union and one of the questions was about their reasons for coming to Turkey, such as marriage; jobs and careers; labor migration; new opportunities; or other reasons.

According to the results of these interviews, the majority of the women (63% of all interviewed women) came to Turkey to marry.

Table 1.1 presents the reasons for women for coming to Turkey.

According to my estimations, the percentages of women who come to Turkey with the aim of marrying are as follows - 20% of Armenian women come to Turkey for marriage; 38% of Azerbaijani women; 82% of Belarusian women; 22% of Georgian women; 62% of Kazakhstani women; 17% of Kyrgyzstani women; 75% of Latvian women; 43% of

Lithuanian women; 60% of Moldovan women; 72% of Russian women; 27% of Turkmenistan women; 66% of Ukrainian women, and 50% of Uzbekistani women.

A large percentage of women come to Turkey to work and for career purposes. Accordingly, 80% of Armenian women come to Turkey to work; 31% of Azerbaijani women; 14% of Belarusian women; 100% of Estonian women; 11% of Georgian women; 23% of Kazakhstani women; 50% of Kyrgyzstani women; 25% of Latvian women; 43% of Lithuanian women; 30% of Moldovan women; 20% of Russian women; 100% of Tajikistani women; 33% of Turkmenistan women; 21% of Ukrainian women, and 40% of Uzbekistani women.

Table 1.1. Showing why women from the countries of the Former Soviet Union came to Turkey according to the results of structured interviews, %

Countries	Marri-age	Jobs and Careers	Labor migra-tion	New opportu-nities	Other reasons
Armenia	20	80	0	0	0
Azerbaijan	38	31	19	6	6
Belarus	82	14	0	14	0
Estonia	0	100	0	0	0
Georgia	22	11	67	0	0
Kazakhstan	62	23	8	0	8
Kyrgyzstan	17	50	17	8	8
Latvia	75	25	0	0	0
Lithuania	43	43	0	14	0
Moldova	60	30	5	5	0
Russia	72	20	3	3	2
Tajikistan	0	100	0	0	0
Turkmenistan	27	33	33	7	0
Ukraine	66	21	7	2	4
Uzbekistan	50	40	10	0	0

Some women also come to Turkey for labor migration: 19% of Azerbaijani women; 67% of Georgian women; 8% of Kazakhstani women; 17% of Kyrgyzstani women; 5% of Moldovan women; 3% of Russian women; 33% of Turkmenistan women; 7% of Ukrainian women, and 10% of Uzbekistani women.

Some of the women come to Turkey seeking new opportunities for themselves: 6% of Azerbaijani women; 14% of Belarusian women; 8% of Kyrgyzstani women; 14% of Lithuanian women; 5% of Moldovan women; 3% of Russian women; 7% of Turkmenistan women; and 2% of

Ukrainian women. Those coming for other reasons are - 6% of Azerbaijani women; 8% of Kazakhstani women; 8% of Kyrgyzstani women; 2% of Russian women; and 4% of Ukrainian women.

I conclude that the majority of women who come to Turkey were seeking marriage. However, some of them will probably change marital status again sometime later because they were born and brought up in a different culture, with different traditions, with a different mentality and see themselves as individuals. It seems they cannot adapt very easily to their new life, new rules and traditions and therefore their marriage can fail.

Current marital status of women from the countries of the Former Soviet Union

As already noted, women have different reasons for coming to Turkey, such as marriage; jobs and careers; labor migration; new opportunities; and other reasons but the main reason for coming to Turkey is marriage; 63% of all interviewed women moved to Turkey to marry. However, women have arrived in the host country at different times, sometimes one, two or even ten years earlier and over time their marital status has changed for various reasons. Some of them are now divorced, some have married and some have been widowed.

I would like to analyze the current marital status of women from the Former Soviet Union countries who came to Turkey for other reasons in Table 1.2. 40% of Armenian women are currently married compared to 86% of Azerbaijani women; 76% of Belarusian women; 50% of Estonian women; 56% of Georgian women; 92% of Kazakhstani women; 42% of Kyrgyzstani women; 25% of Latvian women; 67% of Lithuanian women; 71% of Moldovan women; 83% of Russian women; 45% of Turkmenistan women; 80% of Ukrainian women; and 86% of Uzbekistani women. Thus, a large percentage of women from the countries of the Former Soviet Union have married in Turkey. Overall 77% of women who participated in this scientific research were married.

The percentage of divorced women among the Armenian women was 20% while; Azerbaijani women - 7%; Belarusian women - 12%; Georgian women - 22%; Moldovan women - 19% Russian women - 6%; Turkmenistan women - 9%; Ukrainian women - 8%; and Uzbekistani women - 14%.

Changes in marital statuses are estimated and shown in Table 1.3. Table 1.3 presents these changes of marital status since their arrival from the countries of the Former Soviet Union. I can say with confidence that the number of women from the countries of the Former USSR who would like to marry a Turkish citizen increases day by day.

Table 1.2. Current marital status of women from the Former Soviet Union who came to Turkey for other reasons, %.

Countries	Married	Single	Divorced	Widow
Armenia	40	20	20	20
Azerbaijan	86	0	7	7
Belarus	76	4	12	8
Estonia	50	50	0	0
Georgia	56	11	22	11
Kazakhstan	92	8	0	0
Kyrgyzstan	42	42	0	16
Latvia	25	75	0	0
Lithuania	67	33	0	0
Moldova	71	10	19	0
Russia	83	10	6	1
Turkmenistan	45	27	9	18
Ukraine	80	11	8	1
Uzbekistan	86	0	14	0

The percentage changes of marital status of Belarusian and Latvian women decreased by 6% and 50%, and percentage changes of marital status of women from other countries of the Former USSR were increased by 20% among Armenian women; by 48% among Azerbaijani women; by 50% among Estonian women; by 34% among Georgian women; by 30% among Kazakhstani women; by 25% among Kyrgyzstani women; by 11% among Moldovan and Russian women; by 18% among Turkmenistan women; by 14% among Ukrainian women, and by 36% among Uzbekistani women.

This is means that dynamics of marriage for women from the countries of the Former Soviet Union with Turkish citizens is positive, even where differences in their culture, mentality and traditions exist.

The majority of women, who come to Turkey for other reasons, sooner or later marry Turkish men. This relates not only to single women, but also to divorced women from the countries of the Former Soviet Union who may come with children from a previous marriage or who may leave children in the country of origin and come to Turkey to build new relationships.

As previously noted, through marriage, women from the countries of the Former Soviet Union try to find a more stable and comfortable life in the host country than they had in their countries of origin. They also seek to secure better prospects for their children from previous or current marriages because recent socio-economic development in Turkey has been very promising and is progressing.

Table 1.3. Percentage changes in marital status of women from the countries of the Former Soviet Union, %

Countries	Marriage as a purpose	Current marital status of women	Percentage change - increase or decrease, %
Armenia	20	40	20
Azerbaijan	38	86	48
Belarus	82	76	-6
Estonia	0	50	50
Georgia	22	56	34
Kazakhstan	62	92	30
Kyrgyzstan	17	42	25
Latvia	75	25	-50
Lithuania	43	67	24
Moldova	60	71	11
Russia	72	83	11
Turkmenistan	27	45	18
Ukraine	66	80	14
Uzbekistan	50	86	36

Exploring the percentage of married women from the countries of the Former USSR in Turkey who are married for the first time

The majority of women whom I met when conducting this research were married, or they were new brides, or they were divorced from Turkish men, or they were looking for Turkish men as potential husbands in Turkey.

Among these women were female immigrants who came to Turkey to marry for the first time in their lives. There were also divorced women who came to marry for a second or third time. They came with or without children from previous marriages.

As noted, 77% of women who participated in this scientific project were currently married, among them 40% of Armenian women were currently married; 86% of Azerbaijani women; 76% of Belarusian women; 50% of Estonian women; 56% of Georgian women; 92% of Kazakhstani women; 42% of Kyrgyzstani women; 25% of Latvian women; 67% of Lithuanian women; 71% of Moldovan women; 83% of Russian women; 45% of Turkmenistan women; 80% of Ukrainian women; and 86% of Uzbekistani women. Thus, 77% of women who participated in this study were currently married but not all of them for the first time.

I have calculated the percentage of first time married women, using their responses, and the number of all married women for this calculation I marked as 100%. Therefore, from all these married women (100%), 78% of them are married first time in their lives, and 22% of them are married second or more times in the host country (Table 1.4).

Table 1.4. Percentage of first and further marriages of women from the countries of the Former USSR in Turkey

Countries	Current marital status of women (is an amount per 100%)	Women in their first marriage, %	Women in their 2nd or further marriages, %
Armenia	40	100	0
Azerbaijan	86	92	8
Belarus	76	95	5
Estonia	50	100	0
Georgia	56	80	20
Kazakhstan	92	67	33
Kyrgyzstan	42	80	20
Latvia	25	0	100
Lithuania	67	100	0
Moldova	71	73	27
Russia	83	81	19
Turkmenistan	45	100	0
Ukraine	80	70	30
Uzbekistan	86	67	33
Total	100%	78	22

Among all Armenian women who were currently married in the host country, 100% were married first time. 92% of Azerbaijani women; 95% of Belarusian women; 100% of Estonian women; 80% of Georgian women; 67% of Kazakhstani women; 80% of Kyrgyzstani women; 100% of Lithuanian women; 73% of Moldovan women; 81% of Russian women; 100% of Turkmenistan women; 70% of Ukrainian women; and 67% of Uzbekistani women.

Some of these women were married before their current marriage in the Turkey and the percentage of these women was 8% of Azerbaijani women; 5% of Belarusian women; 20% of Georgian women; 33% of Kazakhstani women; 20% of Kyrgyzstani women; 100% of Latvian women; 27% of Moldovan women; 19% of Russian women; 30% of Ukrainian women; and 33% of Uzbekistani women.

Some of the currently married women in Turkey from the Former USSR have children from their previous marriages and some of these children moved to the host country with their mothers. Others, who are older, did not move with their mothers but stayed in their countries of origin.

Therefore, never married and divorced or widowed women from the countries of the Former Soviet Union move to Turkey to marry Turkish men. These women may also bring their children from their previous marriages.

How do women from the countries of the Former Soviet Union find their Turkish husbands?

Women from the countries of the Former USSR meet Turkish men mainly during tourist tours and seasonal work in Turkey; or in their countries of origin because there are many Turkish companies through building, oil and gas areas of economy; or by the Internet, marriage agencies or through friends or acquaintances (Koshulko, 2015).

According to data from the Ministry of Foreign Affairs of the Republic of Turkey, numerous enterprises and companies with Turkish representation offices abroad have been established between Turkey and the countries of the Former Soviet Union and many Turks found their brides and future wives while working abroad for these companies.

Regarding the relationship between Turkey and Armenia, Turkey wishes to normalize its bilateral relations with Armenia in order to contribute to an atmosphere of comprehensive peace and cooperation in the South Caucasus. Turkish officials are of the opinion that regional cooperation opportunities will encourage the parties towards a settlement.[1]

According to data of the Ministry of Foreign Affairs of the Republic of Turkey, a high level of strategic cooperation exists between Turkey and Azerbaijan: "Turkey and Azerbaijan are in close cooperation in the areas of energy and transport, as well. The two countries have concluded massive regional projects of strategic importance, such as Baku-Tbilisi-Ceyhan Crude Oil Pipeline, Baku-Tbilisi-Erzurum Natural Gas Pipeline and Baku-Tbilisi-Kars Railway Project. Our cooperation in the field of

---

[1] The Ministry of Foreign Affairs of the Republic of Turkey (MOFA). Relations between Turkey and Armenia. Accessed 1 June 2016. http://www.mfa.gov.tr/ relations-between-turkey-and-armenia.en.mfa.

energy is to be further enhanced with the Trans-Anatolian Natural Gas Pipeline (TANAP), which is going to contribute to the security of energy supply on both regional and international scales".[2]

The relationship between Turkey and Belarus is developing as "Turkey is one of the most active countries in terms of investments in Belarus. The total amount of investments by Turkish entrepreneurs and constructors in Belarus is around the level of 1.2 billion USD since 1991, the year when Belarus gained its independence. Turkey ranks third among the countries that invested in Belarus with the aforementioned investment rate. In this context, successful projects undertaken by Turkish real estate companies come to the forefront".[3]

There are active investments between Turkey and Estonia and these allowed the founding of new enterprises and the opening of Turkish representation offices in Estonia: "Total amount of direct investments from Estonia to Turkey in the period of 2002-2015 is 11 million USD; this figure is 2 million USD from Turkey to Estonia in the same period. Turkey is the most preferred destination for Estonian tourists. Around 65,000 tourists from Estonia have visited Turkey in 2015. Nearly 250 Turkish citizens are resident in Estonia".[4]

Turkey and Georgia "have exemplary relations and close cooperation on a wide range of areas from energy to trade and from economy to education and culture": "Turkey ranks the first biggest trade partner of Georgia with a bilateral trade volume of 1.4 billion USD. Turkish and Georgian citizens are able to travel to each other's country with their national identity documents (without passport). Turkey highly values the regional cooperation projects realized so far. Strategic projects such as Baku-Tbilisi-Ceyhan (BTC) Crude Oil Pipeline and Baku-Tbilisi-Erzurum (BTE) Natural Gas Pipeline are of utmost importance for the two countries. Additionally, the timely finalization of the Baku-Tbilisi-Kars (BTK) railway Project will provide a new impetus to regional cooperation".[5]

Between Turkey and Kazakhstan, there is a high level of strategic cooperation in areas such as food sector, medication-chemistry industry,

[2] MOFA. Relations between Turkey and Azerbaijan. Accessed 1 June 2016. http://www.mfa.gov.tr/relations-between-turkey-and-azerbaijan.en.mfa.

[3] MOFA. Relations between Turkey and Belarus. Accessed 1 June 2016. http://www.mfa.gov.tr/relations-between-turkey-and-belarus.en.mfa.

[4] MOFA. Relations between Turkey and Estonia. Accessed 1 June 2016. http://www.mfa.gov.tr/relations-between-turkey-and-estonia.en.mfa.

[5] MOFA. Relations between Turkey and Georgia. Accessed 1 June 2016. http://www.mfa.gov.tr/relations-between-turkey-and-georgia.en.mfa.

construction, hotel management, manufacturing, education and culture:[6] "In Kazakhstan, Turkish entrepreneurs come to the fore particularly in areas such as food sector, medication-chemistry industry, construction, hotel management and manufacturing. The activities of Turkish companies have been growing in construction sector in Kazakhstan day by day. Turkish construction companies in Kazakhstan carried out projects with the value of 1.78 billion Dollars in 2013 and 1.9 billion Dollars in 2014. In 2015, 600 Turkish companies in Kazakhstan undertook some projects with the value of 2.05 billion Dollars. Turkey is the 17th largest investor in Kazakhstan, in terms of capitalization and the 4th largest country in terms of the investments excluding energy sector. Turkish companies provide employment for more than 15,000 people. According to the data of November 2015 of the Central Bank of the Republic of Turkey, the amount of international direct investment from Kazakhstan to Turkey was 681 million Dollars. There are 482 Kazakh-capitalized companies in Turkey as of June 2015. Cooperation on education and culture constitutes another significant dimension of the relations between two countries. About 13.043 students study in the campuses, established in four cities" (Ministry of Foreign Affairs of the Republic of Turkey 2016).

Cooperation exists between Turkey and Kyrgyzstan in political, economic, commercial, military, cultural, educational, health, transportation areas:[7] "The main documents of our strategic partnership today are the "Agreement on Eternal Friendship and Cooperation" signed by the Presidents in 1997, Declaration on the "Turkey and Kyrgyzstan: Together Towards the 21st Century" issued in 1997, and Joint Statement on Establishment of the High Level Strategic Cooperation Council (HLSCC) signed in 2012" (Ministry of Foreign Affairs of the Republic of Turkey 2016).

There is cooperation between Turkey and Latvia in trade, tourism, education and culture as Latvian students study the Turkish language and culture, and many Turkish citizens live in Latvia: "In 2015, the total trade volume between the two countries reached 296 million USD (exports 173 million; imports 123 million). In the period of 2002-2015, total amount of direct investments from Latvia to Turkey is 87 million USD. This figure is 62 million USD from Turkey to Latvia in the same period. Turkey is the most preferred tourism destination for Latvian

---

[6] MOFA. Relations between Turkey and Kazakhstan. Accessed 1 June 2016. http://www.mfa.gov.tr/relations-between-turkey-and-kazakhstan.en.mfa.
[7] MOFA. Relations between Turkey and Kyrgyzstan. Accessed 1 June 2016. http://www.mfa.gov.tr/relations-between-turkey-and-kyrgyzstan.en.mfa.

people. In 2015, more than 60, Latvian tourists visited Turkey. Approximately 90 Turkish citizens are resident in Latvia" (Ministry of Foreign Affairs of the Republic of Turkey 2016).

Turkey and Lithuania's cooperation is in trade, education, tourism, manufacturing and commerce: "The total trade volume between the two countries amounted to 568 million Dollars in 2015. In the period of 2002-2015, total amount of direct investments from Lithuania to Turkey is 22 million USD. This figure is 2 million USD from Turkey to Lithuania in the same period. Turkey is the most preferred touristic destination for Lithuanian people. Around 112 thousand tourists from Lithuania had visited Turkey in 2015. In Lithuania three universities offer Turkish language courses in their curriculum. Approximately 250 Turkish citizens are resident in Lithuania" (Ministry of Foreign Affairs of the Republic of Turkey 2016).

Turkey and Moldova have signed bilateral agreements in trade and commerce: "The bilateral trade volume between Turkey and Moldova in 2012 amounted to 224 million USD of Turkish exports, 135 million USD of imports from Moldova. Turkey attributes particular importance to the relations with the Autonomous Territorial Unit of Gagauzia where live Gagauzians. There are nearly 170,000 Gagauz people are living in Moldova out of which 160,000 live in Gagauzia" (Ministry of Foreign Affairs of the Republic of Turkey 2016).

Turkey and Russia have a large volume of trade relations as many from both countries have companies operating in tourism, construction, the hotel and related services, transportation, oil and gas, trade and manufacturing while also a large number of Russian women married Turkish husbands, and these women are referred to as "Russian Wives" in Turkey.

Relations between Turkey and Tajikistan are marked by friendship and cooperation in the context of Turkey's desire to develop relations with Central Asian Republics following the dissolution of the USSR (Ministry of Foreign Affairs of the Republic of Turkey, 2016).

Regarding the relations between Turkey and Turkmenistan, there is cooperation in diverse fields: foreign policy, trade, economy, culture and education: "In 2015, exports and imports from Turkey to Turkmenistan amounted, respectively, to 1.85 billion USD and 557 million USD. Turkish businessmen have contributed to the development of Turkmenistan since the first days of its independence. Approximately 600 Turkish companies are registered in Turkmenistan. Turkmenistan has become the leading country in the Central Asia for Turkish contracting companies. From the independence of Turkmenistan until today, Turkish contracting companies have carried out more than 1,400 projects worth 47 billion USD. Apart from the construction sector, textile is another field in which Turkish companies operate extensively. Approximately 9,000 Turkish citizens living in Turkmenistan act. Each year, numerous Turkmen citizens visit Turkey for tourism or trade, and thousands of Turkmen students are educated in Turkey. The number of Turkmen visitors in Turkey has been 175,000 in 2015 with an increasing rate of 16% compared to 150,000 visitors in 2013" (Ministry of Foreign Affairs of the Republic of Turkey, 2016).

Turkey and Ukraine are cooperating in political, economic, commercial, construction, touristic, military, cultural, educational, health, and transportation areas: "The total Turkish investments in Ukraine amount to 2 billion USD. Turkish constructors have undertaken projects worth 3.8 billion USD. The Ukrainian tourist arrivals to Turkey surpassed 600,000 visitors. Turkey is the top tourist destination for Ukrainians. The total value of projects realized by the Ukraine Coordinating Office of the Turkish Cooperation and Coordination Agency (TİKA) amounts to 25 million USD. The cooperation in the military sphere is conducted on a bilateral basis as well as within the context of the NATO-Ukraine Commission, BLACKSEAFOR and Operation Blacksea Harmony" (Ministry of Foreign Affairs of the Republic of Turkey 2016).

Turkey and Uzbekistan relations are strong as there are hundreds of companies in Uzbekistan with Turkish capital and represented in the sectors of textile, food, and hotel management, building materials, plastic, medication and service: "The Turkish trade volume with Uzbekistan was 1.2 billion Dollars in 2015. There are currently 700 companies in Uzbekistan with Turkish capital, 100 of which are representation offices. They carry out activities in the sectors of textile, commitment, food, hotel management, building materials, plastic, medication and service. There are 114 companies in Turkey with Uzbek capital" (Ministry of Foreign Affairs of the Republic of Turkey, 2016).

According to the Ministry of Foreign Affairs of the Republic of Turkey, hundreds of enterprises and companies with Turkish capital operate in the countries of the Former Soviet Union, and they employ thousands of Turkish men, and this context allows women from the countries of the Former USSR and Turkish men to meet and marry.

CHAPTER 2

SOCIO-ECONOMICS AND POLITICS IN THE COUNTRIES OF THE FORMER SOVIET UNION AND TURKEY

The 15 countries that gained independence from the Soviet Union are Armenia, Azerbaijan, Belarus, Estonia, Georgia, Kazakhstan, Kyrgyzstan, Latvia, Lithuania, Moldova, Russia, Tajikistan, Turkmenistan, Ukraine, and Uzbekistan. In this chapter, first country profiles of Turkey and the countries of the Former Soviet Union are presented in brief format starting with the countries neighbouring to the east and moving north.

Turkey was defined as "once the centre of the Ottoman Empire, the modern secular republic was established in the 1920s by nationalist leader Kemal Ataturk. Straddling the continents of Europe and Asia, Turkey's strategically important location has given it major influence in the region - and control over the entrance to the Black Sea." [8]

Armenia is "a landlocked country with Turkey to the west and Georgia to the north, Armenia boasts a history longer than most other European countries. Situated along the route of the Great Silk Road, it has fallen within the orbit of a number of cultural influences and empires. After independence from the Soviet Union in 1991, Armenia quickly became drawn into a bloody conflict with Azerbaijan over the mostly Armenian-speaking region of Nagorno-Karabakh. One of the earliest Christian civilisations, its first churches was founded in the fourth century. Unemployment and poverty remain widespread. Armenia's economic problems are aggravated. Despite these problems, Armenia's economy experienced several years of double-digit growth before a sharp downturn set in 2008. Though the economy grew by about 7% in 2012, by the beginning of 2013 more than 30% of the population were still living below the poverty line." [9]

Azerbaijan is an oil-rich country that "has redefined itself over the past two decades from a struggling newly independent state to a major regional energy player. Deals with international energy producers have

---

[8] BBC. 2016. "Turkey country profile." Accessed 5 May 2016. http://www.bbc.com/news/world-europe-17988453.
[9] BBC. 2016. "Armenia country profile." Accessed 5 May 2016. http://www.bbc.com/news/world-europe-17398605.

allowed the country to use its energy revenues to create a government-run fund involved in international projects. In 1994 Azerbaijan signed an oil contract worth $7.4bn with a Western consortium. Since then Western companies have invested millions in the development of the country's oil and gas reserves. Azerbaijan has large gas reserves, and in September 2014 BP began construction of the Southern Gas Corridor to supply Europe directly by 2019, bypassing Russia. Azerbaijan became a member of the Council of Europe in 2001. Often accused of rampant corruption and election-rigging, ruling circles walk a tightrope between Russian and Western regional geo-strategic interests." [10]

Belarus is a country that "in the Soviet post-war years, became one of the most prosperous parts of the USSR, but with independence came economic decline. Private business is virtually non-existent. Foreign investors stay away. The economic situation deteriorated drastically in the summer of 2011 when a balance of payments crisis drained the country's hard-currency reserves. The government's efforts to re-peg the official exchange rate and freeze the price of staple foodstuffs failed to impress either Russia or the International Monetary Fund, to both of which Belarus appealed for assistance." [11]

Estonia "is the most northerly of the three Baltic states, and has linguistic ties with Finland. Since regaining its independence with the collapse of the Soviet Union in 1991, Estonia has become one of the most economically successful of the European Union's newer eastern European members. Estonian governments have tended to pursue strongly free-market economic policies, privatising state enterprises, introducing a flat-rate income tax, liberalising regulation, encouraging free trade and keeping public debt low. There has also been a strong emphasis on making Estonia a world leader in technology, leading some to speak of an "e-economy". This has included creating one of the world's fastest broadband networks, offering widespread free wireless internet, encouraging technology start-ups and putting government services online. In 2007, Estonia was the first country to allow online voting in a general election. The country experienced an investment boom in the early 2000s, especially after EU membership, with high annual growth rates hovering between 7-10%. In 2008, Estonia's economy was hit by the global financial crisis. The government adopted tough austerity measures and won plaudits for getting the economy back

---

[10]   BBC. 2016. "Azerbaijan country profile." Accessed 5 May 2016. http://www.bbc.com/news/world-europe-17043424.
[11]   BBC. 2016. "Belarus country profile." Accessed 5 May 2016. http://www.bbc.com/news/world-europe-17941131.

into shape. The country joined the European single currency in January 2011." [12]

Georgia is significantly impoverished and suffers from corruption and crime. It was "once a relatively affluent part of the USSR, with independence Georgia lost the cheap energy to which it had access in the Soviet period. Since then, it has succeeded in diversifying the sources of its energy supplies, and now receives most of its gas from Azerbaijan." [13]

Kazakhstan is "a huge country the size of Western Europe, Kazakhstan has vast mineral resources and enormous economic potential. The varied landscape stretches from the mountainous, heavily populated regions of the east to the sparsely populated, energy-rich lowlands in the west, and from the industrialised north, with its Siberian climate and terrain, through the arid, empty steppes of the centre, to the fertile south. Ethnically the former Soviet republic is as diverse, with the Kazakhs making up nearly two thirds of the population, ethnic Russians just under a quarter, and smaller minorities the rest. Suppressed under Soviet rule, the main religion, Islam, is undergoing a revival. Since independence following the collapse of the Soviet Union in 1991, major investment in the oil sector has brought rapid economic growth, and eased some of the start disparities in wealth of the 1990s." [14]

Kyrgyzstan is "a Central Asian state bordering China, Kyrgyzstan became independent with the collapse of the Soviet Union in 1991.It has some oil and gas and a developing gold mining sector, but relies on imports for most of its energy needs. Resentment at widespread poverty and ethnic divisions between north and south have spilled over into violence, and the country's first two post-Soviet presidents were swept from power by popular discontent. Most of its six million people are Turkic-speaking Muslims." [15]

Latvia is "situated in north-eastern Europe with a coastline along the Baltic Sea, Latvia has borders with Estonia, Russia, Belarus and Lithuania. It has linguistic links with Lithuania to the south and historical and religious ties with Estonia to the north. Not much more than a decade after it declared independence following the collapse of

---

[12] BBC. 2016. "Estonia country profile." Accessed 5 May 2016. http://www.bbc.com/news/world-europe-17220811.

[13] BBC. 2016. "Georgia country profile." Accessed 5 May 2016. http://www.bbc.com/news/world-europe-17302106.

[14] BBC. 2015. "Kazakhstan country profile." Accessed 5 May 2016. http://www.bbc.com/news/world-asia-pacific-15263826.

[15] BBC. 2016. "Kyrgyzstan country profile." Accessed 5 May 2016. http://www.bbc.com/news/world-asia-16186907.

the USSR, Latvia was welcomed as an EU member in May 2004. The move came just weeks after it joined Nato. For centuries Latvia was primarily an agricultural country, with seafaring, fishing and forestry as other important factors in its economy. Like its Baltic neighbours, in the decade after independence Latvia made a rapid transformation to embrace the free market." [16]

Lithuania "is the largest and most southerly of the three Baltic republics. Not much more than a decade after it regained its independence during the collapse of the Soviet Union in 1990, Lithuania was welcomed as a Nato member in late March 2004.The move came just weeks before a second historic shift for the country in establishing its place in the Western family of nations as it joined the EU in May 2004. These developments would have been extremely hard to imagine in not-so-distant Soviet times." [17]

Moldova is "sandwiched between Romania and Ukraine, Moldova emerged as an independent republic following the collapse of the Soviet Union in 1991. Moldova is one of the poorest countries in Europe, with its economy relying heavily on agriculture. Two-thirds of Moldovans are of Romanian descent. The languages are virtually identical and the two countries share a common cultural heritage. The industrialised territory to the east of the Dniester, generally known as Trans-Dniester or the Dniester region, was formally an autonomous area within Ukraine before 1940, when the Soviet Union combined it with Bessarabia to form the Moldavian Soviet Socialist Republic." [18]

Russia has "emerged from a decade of post-Soviet economic and political turmoil to reassert itself as a world power. Russia's recent economic power has lain in its key natural resources - oil and gas. A long economic boom based on high oil and gas prices started to end in 2013, when Russia's economic prospects began to worsen. This was exacerbated by a sharp fall in world oil prices and the imposition of Western sanctions the following year. Some observers say the root cause is that the economy is still too dependent on raw material exports." [19]

[16] BBC. 2016. "Latvia country profile." Accessed 5 May 2016. http://www.bbc.com/news/world-europe-17522134.

[17] BBC. 2016. "Lithuania country profile." Accessed 5 May 2016. http://www.bbc.com/news/world-europe-17536867.

[18] BBC. 2016. "Moldova country profile." Accessed 5 May 2016. http://www.bbc.com/news/world-europe-17536867.

[19] BBC. 2016. "Russia country profile." Accessed 5 May 2016. http://www.bbc.com/news/world-europe-17839672.

Tajikistan "has never really recovered from the civil war, and poverty is widespread. Almost half of GDP is earned by migrants working abroad, especially in Russia, but the recession in 2009 threatened that income. The country is also dependent on oil and gas imports. Economic hardship is seen as a contributing to a renewed interest in Islam - including more radical forms - among young Tajiks. Tajikistan has relied heavily on Russian assistance to counter continuing security problems and cope with the dire economic situation. Skirmishes with drug smugglers crossing illegally from Afghanistan occur regularly, as Tajikistan is the first stop on the drugs route from there to Russia and the West. Economic ties with neighbouring China are extensive. China has extended credits and has helped to build roads, tunnels and power infrastructure. Chinese firms are investing in oil and gas exploration and in gold mining." [20]

Turkmenistan is "known for its autocratic government and large gas reserves, Turkmenistan also has a reputation as an island of stability in restive Central Asia. Despite its gas wealth, much of Turkmenistan's population is still impoverished. After independence from the Soviet Union in 1991 the country entered a period of isolation that has only recently begun to end. Turkmenistan produces roughly 70 billion cubic metres of natural gas each year and about two-thirds of its exports go to Russia's Gazprom gas monopoly. The government has sought out gas deals with several other countries, including China and neighbouring Iran, however, to reduce its dependency on Russia." [21]

Ukraine is "gained independence after the collapse of the Soviet Union in 1991 and has since veered towards seeking closer integration with Western Europe. Europe's second largest country, Ukraine is a land of wide, fertile agricultural plains, with large pockets of heavy industry in the east." [22]

Uzbekistan is "emerged as a sovereign country after more than a century of Russian rule - first as part of the Russian Empire and then as a component of the Soviet Union. The country is one of the world's biggest producers of cotton and is rich in natural resources, including oil,

---

[20] BBC. 2015. "Tajikistan country profile." Accessed 5 May 2016. http://www.bbc.com/news/world-asia-16201032.
[21] BBC. 2015. "Turkmenistan country profile." Accessed 5 May 2016. http://www.bbc.com/news/world-asia-16094646.
[22] BBC. 2016. "Ukraine country profile." Accessed 5 May 2016. http://www.bbc.com/news/world-europe-18006246.

gas and gold. However, economic reform has been slow and poverty and unemployment are widespread." [23]

Even these brief profiles are indicative of the problems and struggles in these countries of the Former Soviet Union. Povery and unemployment are known to be reasons for female migration to Turkey from these countries.

Indexes of socio-economic development: Turkey and the countries of the Former Soviet Union

The socio-economic development of Turkey and the countries of the Former Soviet Union are different and here it is necessary to explain why female migrants from the countries of the Former USSR would like to migrate from their countries to Turkey.

Indexes that will be analysed in this chapter are the Human Development Index of Turkey and the countries of the Former Soviet Union; Minimum Monthly Wages of these countries; GDP per capita of the countries; their levels of Economic Growth (GDP, their annual variation in %); and Purchasing power parity (PPP).

The first index to be analyzed is the Human Development Index. What is the Human Development Index?

According to the newspaper "The Economic Times: Business News, Personal Finance, Financial News" the Human Development Index is "a statistical tool used to measure a country's overall achievement in its social and economic dimensions" (The Economic Times, 2016): "The social and economic dimensions of a country are based on the health of people, their level of education attainment and their standard of living". Therefore, according to data from the United Nations Development Programme (UNDP), the Human Development Reports from 2014 (United Nations Development Programme 2014), [24] some of the countries of the Former Soviet Union in 2014 had a very high Human Development Index (HDI). These countries were Estonia - 0.861; Lithuania - 0.839; and Latvia - 0.819 (Table 2.1).

In 2014, Turkey and some of the countries of the Former Soviet Union had a high Human Development Index (HDI). These countries were Belarus - 0.798; Russian Federation - 0.798; Kazakhstan - 0.788; Turkey - 0.761; Georgia - 0.754; Azerbaijan - 0.751; Ukraine - 0.747;

---

[23] BBC. 2015. "Uzbekistan country profile." Accessed 5 May 2016. http://www.bbc.com/news/world-asia-16218112.

[24] UNDP - United Nations Development Programme. 2014. "Human Development Reports." Accessed 13 May 2016. http://hdr.undp.org/en/composite/HDI.

and Armenia - 0.733. Some of the countries of the Former Soviet Union in 2014 had a medium Human Development Index (HDI). These countries were Moldova - 0.693; Turkmenistan - 0.688; Uzbekistan - 0.675; Kyrgyzstan - 0.655; and Tajikistan - 0.624. No countries of the Former Soviet Union appeared among the countries with a low Human Development Index (HDI) in 2014.

Table 2.1. Human Development Index (HDI): Turkey and the countries of the Former Soviet Union

HDI rank in 2014	HDI	Countries
Countries with the very high Human Development Index		
30	0.861	Estonia
37	0.839	Lithuania
46	0.819	Latvia
Countries with the high Human Development Index		
50	0.798	Belarus
50	0.798	Russian Federation
56	0.788	Kazakhstan
72	0.761	Turkey
76	0.754	Georgia
78	0.751	Azerbaijan
81	0.747	Ukraine
85	0.733	Armenia
Countries with the medium Human Development Index		
107	0.693	Moldova
109	0.688	Turkmenistan
114	0.675	Uzbekistan
120	0.655	Kyrgyzstan
129	0.624	Tajikistan

The HDI rankings in the Human Development Reports from 2014, Estonia (0.861); Lithuania (0.839); and Latvia (0.819) had the highest HDI ranking among the countries of the Former Soviet Union and very high Human Development Index (HDI) among all the ranked countries. Estonia had an HDI ranking of 0.861 and was No.30 in the rankings in 2014 among 188 countries of the world. Lithuania had an HDI ranking of 0.839 and was No.37 in the overall rankings. Latvia had an HDI ranking of 0.819 and was No.46 in the overall rankings in 2014.

Turkey and some of the countries of the Former Soviet Union had a high Human Development Index (HDI) ranking with scores between 0.798 and 0.733. Thus, Belarus and Russian Federation had an HDI ranking - 0.798 and was No.50 in the overall HDI rankings in 2014. Kazakhstan had an HDI ranking of 0.788 and was No.56 in the overall

HDI rankings. Turkey had 0.761 in the HDI rankings and was No.72 overall HDI. Georgia had 0.754 as its HDI rank and was No.76 in the overall HDI rankings. Azerbaijan had 0.751 as its HDI rank and was No.78 in the overall HDI rankings. Ukraine had 0.747 as its HDI rank and was No.81 in the overall HDI rankings; and Armenia had 0.733 as its HDI rank and was No.85 in the overall HDI rankings in 2014.

Some of the countries of the Former Soviet Union were ranked as medium in the Human Development Index (HDI), and among these countries were Moldova with an HDI ranking of 0.693 and No.107 in the overall rankings in 2014; Turkmenistan with an HDI ranking of 0.688 and No.109 in the overall rankings; Uzbekistan with an HDI ranking of 0.675 and No.114 in the overall rankings; Kyrgyzstan with an HDI ranking of 0.655 and No.120 in the overall rankings; and Tajikistan with an HDI ranking of 0.624 and No.129 in the overall ranking.

Therefore, female migrant flows to Turkey from the countries of the Former Soviet Union with a very high Human Development Index (HDI) like Estonia; Lithuania; and Latvia are minimal because the HDI ranking of these counties in 2014 was higher than that of Turkey.

According to the Human Development Index Reports of 2014, countries with a higher HDI rank than Turkey were Belarus and Russian Federation (No.50 in the HDI ranking in 2014); and Kazakhstan (No.56 in the HDI ranking). Turkey was No.72 in the HDI ranking. The other countries of the Former Soviet Union had lower HDI rankings than Turkey and this explains the large female migration flows from the other countries of the Former Soviet Union to Turkey.

So, according to the Human Development Index Report from 2014, the highest HDI rankings among the countries of the Former Soviet Union were for Estonia, Lithuania, and Latvia, and the lowest HDI rankings among these countries were in Uzbekistan, Kyrgyzstan and Tajikistan.

Current development level of Turkey and the countries of the Former Soviet Union

I would like to explain the desire of citizens of the countries of the Former Soviet Union to migrate from their countries of origin to other host countries, in particular, to Turkey.

The comparison of some of the economic data of these 15 independent countries, including minimum monthly wages and the GDP per capita of the countries; their level of Economic Growth (GDP, annual variation in %), will explain, why migration flows from the countries of the Former Soviet Union to Turkey already exist and are continuing to develop.

The minimum monthly wages of the countries of the Former Soviet Union and Turkey and the percentage change - increase or decrease - have been analysed thanks to statistics published by Eurostat (Eurostat 2016), and Trading Economics (Trading Economics 2016). The countries of the Former Soviet Union have lower minimum monthly wages than Turkey. I have prepared a comparison of minimum monthly wages in the national currency of the countries of the Former Soviet Union and Turkey in 2015-2016 (see Table 2.2).

The official currency of Republic of Turkey is the Turkish Lira (TL, TRY, Turk Lirası). The Armenian national currency is the Armenian Dram (AMD). The Azerbaijani National Currency is the Azerbaijani manat (AZN). The official currency of Belarus is the Belarusian Ruble (BYR).

Table 2.2. Minimum monthly wages in national currency: Former USSR countries and Turkey in 2015-2016

Countries	2015	2016	Increasing wages in %
Turkey (TRY)	1273.50	1647	22.7
Armenia (AMD)	50000	55000	9.09
Azerbaijan (AZN)	105	105	0
Belarus (BYR)	2100100	2300000	8.69
Estonia (€)	390	430	9.3
Georgia (GEL)	115	115	0
Kazakhstan (KZT)	21364	22859	6.54
Kyrgyzstan (KGS)	940	940	0
Latvia (€)	360	370	2.7
Lithuania (LTL/€)	325	350	7.14
Moldova (MDL)	1900	1900	0
Russia (RUB)	5965	6204	3.85
Tajikistan (TJS)	250	400	37.5
Turkmenistan (TMT)	535	590	9.32
Ukraine (UAH)	1218	1378	11.6
Uzbekistan (UZS)	118400	130240	9.09

Estonia has become the first of the Former Soviet Union countries and 17th European nation to adopt the Euro (EUR; €), and the Euro is now the only official currency in Estonia. The Georgian Lari (GEL) is the currency of Georgia. The Kazakhstani Tenge (KZT) is the currency of Kazakhstan. The Kyrgyzstani som (KGS) is the official currency in Kyrgyzstan. The official currency of Latvia is the Euro (EUR; €) since

1st January 2014, and on 1 January 2015 Lithuania adopted the Euro as its official currency (EUR; €).

The Moldovan Leu (MDL) is the currency of Moldova. The Russian Ruble (or Rouble) (RUB) is the official currency of the Russian Federation. The Tajikistani somoni (TJS) is the currency of Tajikistan. The Turkmenistan Manat (TMT) is the currency of Turkmenistan. The Ukrainian Hryvnia (UAH) is the currency of Ukraine. The national currency of Uzbekistan is the Uzbekistani Som (UZS).

An increase of the minimum monthly wages in the national currencies of the Former Soviet Union countries and Turkey in 2015-2016 occurred in the majority of the countries. The increase of the minimum monthly wage of the Republic of Turkey in 2016 in the national currency was 22.7%. The Armenian minimum monthly wage increased by 9.09%. The Belarusian minimum monthly wage increased by 8.69%. The Estonian minimum monthly wage increased by 9.3%. The increase of the Kazakhstani minimum monthly wage in 2016 was 6.54%. The Latvian minimum monthly wage increased by 2.7%, and the Lithuanian minimum monthly wage increased by 7.14%. The increase of the Russian minimum monthly wage in the national currency was 3.85%. Forecasts for Tajikistani minimum monthly wage increases are 37.5% in 2016. The increase of the Turkmenistan minimum monthly wage will be 9.32%, the Uzbekistani minimum monthly wages will increase by 9.09%, and the Ukrainian minimum monthly wage will increase by 11.6%.

In order to understand the difference between minimum monthly wages of the countries, I will use XE - The World's Trusted Currency Authority[25] (XE 2016), where I convert the minimum monthly wage amount of the Former Soviet Union countries into the Euro (€) (see Table 2.3).

According to my computations, the minimum monthly wage of the Republic of Turkey in 2016 in the Euro is 516.447 EUR (€). The Armenian minimum monthly wage is 100.902 EUR. The Azerbaijani minimum monthly wage is 56.7937 EUR. The Belarusian minimum monthly wage is 99.90614 EUR, and the Estonian minimum monthly wage is 430 EUR.

The Georgian minimum monthly wage is 42.8422 EUR. The Kazakhstani minimum monthly wage is 59.8000 EUR. The minimum

---

[25] XE - The World's Trusted Currency Authority. Accessed March, 2016. http://www.xe.com/.

monthly wage in Kyrgyzstan is 11.6459 EUR. The Latvian minimum monthly wage is 370 EUR, and the Lithuanian minimum monthly wage is 350 EUR. The Moldovan minimum monthly wage in 2016 is 86.1231 EUR. The Russian minimum monthly wage is 79.9200 EUR. The Tajikistani minimum monthly wage is 45.7196 EUR. The Turkmenistan minimum monthly wage is 151.571 EUR. The Ukrainian minimum monthly wage is 48.5921 EUR, and the Uzbekistani minimum monthly wage is 41.0206 EUR.

Table 2.3. Conversion of minimum monthly wages from national currency of the Former Soviet Union countries and Turkey into the EUR (€) in 2015-2016

Countries	2015	EUR (€)	2016	EUR (€)
Turkey (TRY)	1273.50	399.304	1647	516.447
Armenia (AMD)	50000	91.7293	55000	100.902
Azerbaijan (AZN)	105	56.7937	105	56.7937
Belarus (BYR)	2100100	91.22299	2300000	99.90614
Estonia (€)	390	390	430	430
Georgia (GEL)	115	42.8422	115	42.8422
Kazakhstan (KZT)	21364	55.8890	22859	59.8000
Kyrgyzstan (KGS)	940	11.6459	940	11.6459
Latvia (€)	360	360	370	370
Lithuania (€)	325	325	350	350
Moldova (MDL)	1900	86.1231	1900	86.1231
Russia (RUB)	5965	76.8412	6204	79.9200
Tajikistan (TJS)	250	28.5747	400	45.7196
Turkmenistan (TMT)	535	137.441	590	151.571
Ukraine (UAH)	1218	42.9516	1378	48.5921
Uzbekistan (UZS)	118400	37.2820	130240	41.0206

Based on these computations (see Table 2.3) it is possible to create a list of the countries of the Former Soviet Union with the highest and the lowest minimum monthly wage in 2016 and compare these to Turkey. Based on this list I will rank five groups of the countries of the Former Soviet Union from highest to lowest minimum monthly wage according to the minimum monthly wage of Turkey in 2016 (see Table 2.4).

The first group of this ranking consists of the three Baltic countries in northern Europe: Estonia (minimum monthly wage is 430 EUR in 2016); Latvia (370 EUR); and Lithuania (350 EUR). The Turkish minimum monthly wage in 2016 exceeds that of the Baltic countries. The minimum monthly wage of Turkey exceeds the minimum monthly wage of Estonia by 16.7%; Latvia by 28.4%; and Lithuania by 32.2%.

The second group of the ranking consists of the next three countries-Turkmenistan (151.57 EUR); Armenia (100.9 EUR); and Belarus (99.91 EUR). The minimum monthly wage of Turkey (516.45 EUR) in 2016 is 3 to 5 times higher than that of Turkmenistan, Armenia, and Belarus in 2016: 3.4 times higher than the Turkmenistan; 5.1 times higher the Armenian minimum monthly wage; and 5.2 times higher than the Belarusian minimum monthly wage.

Table 2.4. The ranking of five groups of the countries of the Former Soviet Union from the highest to the lowest minimum monthly wages compared to the minimum monthly wage of Turkey in 2016 in EUR (€)

Groups of the ranking	Countries	EUR (€)
	Turkey (TRY)	516.45
The first group of the ranking		
1	Estonia (€)	430
	Latvia (€)	370
	Lithuania (€)	350
The second group of the ranking		
2	Turkmenistan (TMT)	151.57
	Armenia (AMD)	100.9
	Belarus (BYR)	99.91
The third group of the ranking		
3	Moldova (MDL)	86.12
	Russia (RUB)	79.92
	Kazakhstan (KZT)	59.80
The fourth group of the ranking		
4	Azerbaijan (AZN)	56.79
	Ukraine (UAH)	48.59
	Tajikistan (TJS)	45.72
The fifth group of the ranking		
5	Georgia (GEL)	42.84
	Uzbekistan (UZS)	41.02
	Kyrgyzstan (KGS)	11.65

The third group of the ranking consists of the following countries of the Former Soviet Union, Moldova (86.12 EUR); Russia (79.92 EUR); and Kazakhstan (59.80 EUR). Tthe minimum monthly wage of Turkey is 6 to 9 times higher than that of Moldova; Russia; and Kazakhstan in 2016. The minimum monthly wage of Turkey is 6.0 times higher than the Moldavian; 6.5 times higher than the Russian; and 8.6 times higher than the Kazakhstani minimum montly wage.

The fourth group consists of the three following countries of the Former Soviet Union with lower minimum monthly wages, Azerbaijan

(56.79 EUR); Ukraine (48.59 EUR); and Tajikistan (45.72 EUR). The minimum monthly wage of Turkey is 9.1 times higher than that of Azerbaijan; 10.6 times higher than that of Ukraine; and 11.3 times higher than that of Tajikistan in 2016.

Finally, the last, fifth group of the ranking consists of the three following countries of the Former Soviet Union with the lowest minimum minimum monthly wage compared to Turkey. These countries are Georgia (42.84 EUR); Uzbekistan (41.02 EUR); and Kyrgyzstan (11.65 EUR). The minimum monthly wage of Turkey is 12 to 44 times higher than that of Georgia; Uzbekistan; and Kyrgyzstan in 2016. Thus, the minimum monthly wage of Turkey is 12.1 times higher than the Georgian; 12.6 times higher than the Uzbekistani; and 44.3 times higher than the Kyrgyzstani minimum monthly wage in 2016.

According to my computations, the highest minimum monthly wage among the countries of the Former Soviet Union has been set in Estonia, 430 EUR in 2016, and the lowest minimum monthly wage among the countries is in Kyrgyzstan, 940 KGS or 11.65 EUR per month, while the minimum wage of Turkey exceeds even the highest minimum monthly wage among the other countries.

Hence, I conclude, that women from the countries of the Former Soviet Union - where in 2016 minimum monthly wages are 3 to 44 times lower than the minimum monthly wage of Turkey (516.45 EUR), - [these countries are Turkmenistan (151.57 EUR), Armenia (100.9 EUR); Moldova (86.12 EUR); Russia (79.92 EUR); Kazakhstan (59.80 EUR); Azerbaijan (56.79 EUR); Ukraine (48.59 EUR); Tajikistan (45.72 EUR); Georgia (42.84 EUR); Uzbekistan (41.02 EUR); and Kyrgyzstan (11.65 EUR)],- come to Turkey primarily for social-economical reasons.

Thus, migration flows from these countries to Turkey will continue because female migrants seek a better standard of living and quality of life in Turkey. The women try to find a way of bettering their lives and those of their current or future children through marriage, employment or education in Turkey with the intention of staying permanently in the host country.

Exploring GDP per capita and indicators of Economic Growth for Turkey and the countries of the Former Soviet Union

Equally important indicators of socio-economic development of the countries of the Former Soviet Union and Turkey are GDP per capita and a measure of economic growth (Table 2.5).

Table 2.5 presents indicators of socio-economic development of the countries of the Former Soviet Union and Turkey in 2015 as number of population of each country (million); GDP per capita (USD) of each country and level of Economic Growth (GDP, annual variation in %) of the countries in 2015.

Table 2.5. Indicators of socio-economic development of the countries of the Former Soviet Union and Turkey in 2015

Countries	GDP per capita (USD)	Economic Growth (GDP, annual variation in %)
Turkey	9,221	4.0
Armenia	3,241	3.0
Azerbaijan	3,679	1.1
Belarus	6,030	-3.9
Estonia	17,256	1.1
Georgia	3,168	2.8
Kazakhstan	6,768	1.2
Kyrgyzstan	970	3.5
Latvia	13,424	2.7
Lithuania	14,169	1.6
Moldova	1,831	-0.5
Russia	8,181	-3.7
Tajikistan	813	6.0
Turkmenistan	4,092	6.7
Ukraine	2,038	-9.9
Uzbekistan	2,143	8.0

Source: Focus Economics and Ieconomics

According to the Conference Board of Canada, income per capita is the most frequently used statistic for comparing economic well-being across countries: "It is calculated as gross domestic product (GDP) per capita - it is not a measure of personal income. Therefore, income per capita measures the value of goods and services exchanged in the marketplace. High performance in this category, either in terms of growth or the level of per capita income, does not guarantee a high quality of life. Nevertheless, a country that is not generating enough income for its citizens are hampered in what it can do on the environmental and social fronts" (Conference Board of Canada, 2016).

As a measure of the total output of a country divided by the number of people resident in that country, "the per capita GDP is especially useful when comparing one country to another because it shows the relative performance of the countries. A rise in per capita GDP signals growth in the economy and tends to translate as an increase in productivity" (Investopedia, 2016).

In 2015, Turkey had GDP per capita of 9,221 dollars (USD), higher than in the majority of the countries of the Former Soviet Union. From all the countries of the Former Soviet Union in 2015 only the Baltic countries, Estonia, Lithuania, and Latvia (17,256 USD; 14,169 USD; and 13424 USD) had higher GDP per capita than in Turkey.

The lowest GDP per capita figures occurred in the following countries of the Former Soviet Union in 2015:- in Russia - GDP per capita was 8,181 USD; Kazakhstan – 6,768 USD; Belarus – 6,030 USD; Turkmenistan – 4,092 USD; Azerbaijan – 3,679 USD; Armenia - 3241 USD; Georgia – 3,168 USD; Uzbekistan – 2,143 USD; Ukraine – 2,038 USD; Moldova – 1,831 USD; Kyrgyzstan - 970 USD; and Tajikistan - 813 USD.

Figure 2.1. Economic Growth (GDP, annual variation in %) of the countries of the Former Soviet Union and Turkey in 2015

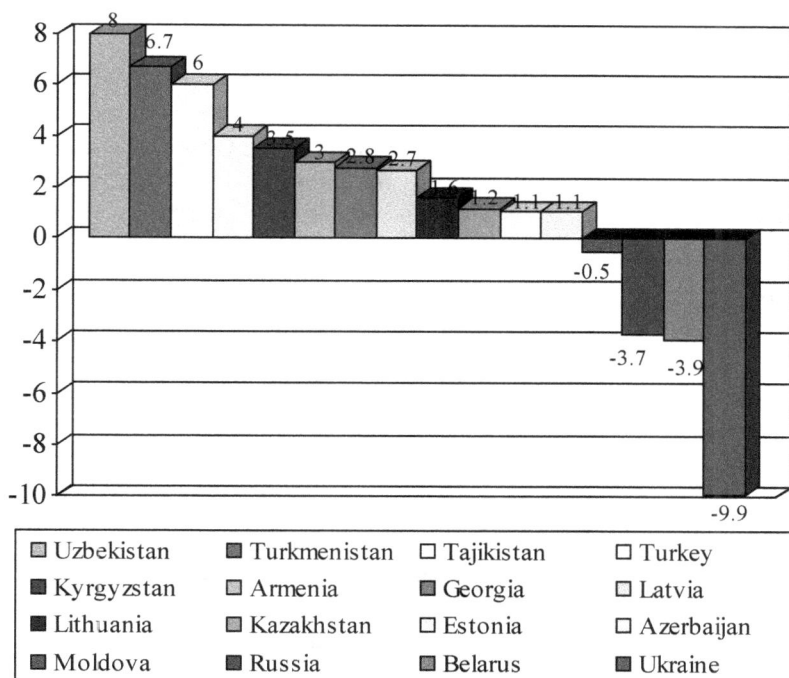

☐ Uzbekistan	■ Turkmenistan	☐ Tajikistan	☐ Turkey
■ Kyrgyzstan	☐ Armenia	☐ Georgia	☐ Latvia
■ Lithuania	☐ Kazakhstan	☐ Estonia	☐ Azerbaijan
☐ Moldova	■ Russia	☐ Belarus	■ Ukraine

Source: Focus Economics: Economic Indicators, News and Forecasts

According to data from Focus Economics: Economic Indicators, News and Forecasts, Economic Growth in Turkey in 2015 (GDP, annual variation in %) was 4.0% (Focus Economics 2016) [Figure 2.1]. On the basis of data of the Economic Growth (GDP, annual variation in %) of

15 independent countries of the Former Soviet Union it is possible to analyze the level of socio-economic progress in these countries compared with Turkey in 2015.

According to Focus Economics, the highest level of Economic Growth (GDP, annual variation in %) among the countries of the Former Soviet Union was in 2015 in Uzbekistan - 8.0%, and the lowest level of Economic Growth (GDP, annual variation in %) was in 2015 in Ukraine - (-9.9%) due to the undeclared war in that country throughout the last two years.

Higher levels of Economic Growth (GDP, annual variation in %) than in Turkey in 2015 occurred in Turkmenistan (6.7%) and Tajikistan (6.0%), but all other countries had a lower level of Economic Growth (GDP, annual variation in %) than in Turkey in 2015.

Present socio-economic situation in Turkey and in the countries of the Former Soviet Union

The three Baltic countries in northern Europe, Estonia, Latvia, and Lithuania have similar and very high indicators compared to Turkish indicators of socio-economic development. Currently these countries are part of the EU and their minimum monthly wages, GDP per capita, and the level of Economic Growth (GDP, annual variation in %) are high in comparison to other countries of the Former Soviet Union.

Thus, a lower percentage of women from the Baltic countries in northern Europe come to Turkey for socio-economic reasons. In my opinion, women from the other countries of the Former Soviet Union where the minimum monthly wages are lower than the Turkish minimum monthly wage (516.45 EUR), [for example, 3 times lower in Turkmenistan 151.57 EUR and, significantly, 44 times lower in Kyrgyzstan 11.65 EUR in 2016] come to Turkey with the primary desire of finding better standards of life there than in their countries of origin. Their secondary desire is to work or marry there.

Analysis of the GDP per capita and Economic Growth of Turkey and the countries of the Former Soviet Union show that Estonia, Lithuania, and Latvia had GDP per capita higher than Turkey in 2015.

All other countries of the Former Soviet Union had a lower GDP per capita than Turkey in 2015, which explains why Turkey is so attractive to women from the countries of the Former Soviet Union.

I conclude that women from the countries of the Former Soviet Union where minimum monthly wages, the GDP per capita and level of Economic Growth (GDP, annual variation in %) are lower than these same indicators in Turkey, try to find a way of improving their lives through marriage, employment or education in Turkey with the intention of staying permanently.

Using minimum monthly wages, GDP per capita, and the level of Economic Growth (GDP, annual variation in %), I conclude that migration flows from the countries of the Former Soviet Union to Turkey will continue because female migrants seek a better standard of living and quality of life in Turkey and try to find a way of bettering their lives and those of their current and future children through marriage, employment or education in Turkey with the intention of staying there permanently.

In the next section, I would like to discuss the GDP per capita at Purchasing Power Parity in the countries of the Former Soviet Union and in Turkey (PPP GDP or PPP).

Purchasing Power Parities of the countries of the Former Soviet Union and Turkey

I would also like to compare the GDP at Purchasing Power Parity in Turkey and in the countries of the Former Soviet Union. An earlier study looked into the Common wealth of Independent States, but only 6 of 15 countries of the Former Soviet Union, Armenia, Belarus, Georgia, Kazakhstan, Kyrgyzstan and Russia, were studied there (Pehlivan, 2014). What is GDP at Purchasing power parity (PPP or PPP GDP)? Purchasing power parity (PPP or PPP GDP) is: "…a theory in economics that approximates the total adjustment that must be made on the currency exchange rate between countries that allows the exchange to be equal to the purchasing power of each country's currency. To make a comparison of prices across countries that hold any type of meaning, a wide range of goods and services must be considered. The amount of data that must be collected, and the complexity of drawing comparisons, makes this process difficult. Using PPPs is the alternative to using market exchange rates. The actual purchasing power of any currency is the quantity of that currency needed to buy a specified unit of a good or a basket of common goods and services. PPP is determined in each country based on its relative cost of living and inflation rates. Purchasing power plus parity ultimately means equalizing the purchasing power of two differing currencies by accounting for differences in inflation rates and cost of living" (Investopedia, 2016).

According to the article "Definition of the Purchasing Power Parity" by "The Economic Times: Business News, Personal Finance, and Financial News", "PPP is used worldwide to compare the income levels in different countries. PPP thus makes it easy to understand and interpret the data of each country" (The Economic Times, 2016).

I would like to compare Turkey and the countries of the Former Soviet Union on basis of data from the World Bank (in current international $). Using the data of the Purchasing Power Parity of Turkey and the countries of the Former Soviet Union it is possible to see the gap that exists between Turkey and countries of the Former Soviet Union. Table 2.6 presents a comparison of the PPP GDP or the PPP in U.S. dollars on the basis of data from the World Bank in 2014.

Table 2.6. Showing the Purchasing Power Parity of Turkey and the countries of the Former Soviet Union on the basis of data from the World Bank (in current international $) in 2014

Countries	PPP GDP	Countries	PPP GDP
Turkey	19,787.7	Latvia	23,547.9
Armenia	8,069.7	Lithuania	27,685.9
Azerbaijan	17,520.7	Moldova	4,982.6
Belarus	18,184.9	Russia	22,989.6
Estonia	28,139.9	Tajikistan	2,690.8
Georgia	9,162.9	Turkmenistan	15,473.6
Kazakhstan	24,227.7	Ukraine	8,665.5
Kyrgyzstan	3,321.5	Uzbekistan	5,573.1

Source: Data of the World Bank Group

According to the definition of the World Bank, the PPP GDP is gross domestic product converted to international dollars using purchasing power parity rates (World Bank, 2016). Data of the World Bank enables the ranking of the PPP GDP for Turkey and the countries of the Former Soviet Union in Table 2.7.

Based on data from the World Bank Group (see Table 2.6) it is possible to create a ranking of the PPP GDP of the countries of the Former Soviet Union with the highest and the lowest PPP GDP in 2014 in relation to Turkey. I have created a ranking of five groups of the countries of the Former Soviet Union from the highest to the lowest PPP GDP according to the PPP GDP of Turkey in 2014 (see Table 2.7).

The first group of this ranking consists of Estonia (the PPP GDP is $28,139.9 in 2014); Lithuania ($27,685.9); and Kazakhstan ($24,227.7). The Turkish PPP GDP did not exceed the PPP GDP of these three countries in 2014.

The second group of the ranking consists of the next three countries Latvia ($23,547.9); Russia ($22,989.6); and Belarus ($18,184.9).

The third group of the ranking consists of the following countries of the Former Soviet Union - Azerbaijan ($17,520.7); Turkmenistan ($15,473.6); and Georgia ($9,162.9).

The fourth group consists of the three following countries of the Former Soviet Union - Ukraine ($8,665.5); Armenia ($8,069.7), and Uzbekistan ($5,573.1).

The last, fifth group of the ranking consists of the three following countries of the Former Soviet Union with the lowest PPP GDP compared to Turkey. These countries are Moldova ($4,982.6); Kyrgyzstan ($3,321.5); and Tajikistan ($2,690.8).

Table 2.7. Showing a ranking of the PPP GDP for Turkey and the countries of the Former Soviet Union in 2014 (in current international $)

Ranking	Countries	PPP GDP	Ranking	Countries	PPP GDP
Turkey	19,787.7				
1	Estonia	28,139.9	9	Georgia	9,162.9
2	Lithuania	27,685.9	10	Ukraine	8,665.5
3	Kazakhstan	24,227.7	11	Armenia	8,069.7
4	Latvia	23,547.9	12	Uzbekistan	5,573.1
5	Russia	22,989.6	13	Moldova	4,982.6
6	Belarus	18,184.9	14	Kyrgyzstan	3,321.5
7	Azerbaijan	17,520.7	15	Tajikistan	2,690.8
8	Turkmenistan	15,473.6	Total 15 countries and Turkey		

Source: Data of the World Bank Group

According to my computations, the highest PPP GDP among the countries of the Former Soviet Union has been set in Estonia, and the lowest PPP GDP among the countries is in Tajikistan.

In this chapter some indexes, including the Human Development Index of Turkey and the countries of the Former Soviet Union; minimum monthly wages of the countries; GDP per capita of the countries; their level of Economic Growth (GDP, annual variation in %); and the Purchasing power parity (PPP or PPP GDP) have been analyzed.

According to the HDI rank of the Human Development Reports from 2014, the highest HDI ranks among the countries of the Former Soviet Union have been set in Estonia, Lithuania, and Latvia, and the lowest HDI ranks among these countries are in Uzbekistan, Kyrgyzstan and Tajikistan.

The highest minimum monthly wage among the countries of the Former Soviet Union has been set in Estonia, 430 EUR in 2016, and the lowest minimum monthly wage among the countries is in Kyrgyzstan,

940 KGS or 11.65 EUR per month, while the minimum wage of Turkey exceeds even the highest minimum monthly wage among the other countries.

The highest level of Economic Growth (GDP, annual variation in %) among the countries of the Former Soviet Union was in 2015 in Uzbekistan - 8.0%, and the lowest level of Economic Growth (GDP, annual variation in %) was in 2015 in Ukraine - (-9.9%) due to the undeclared war in the country during the last two years.

In the cases where the Human Development Index, minimum monthly wages, the GDP per capita, and level of Economic Growth (GDP, annual variation in %) are lower than these same indicators in Turkey, women from the countries of the Former Soviet Union try to find a way of improving their lives through marriage, employment or education in Turkey with the intention of staying in the country permanently.

So, using my rankings and computations of the Human Development Index, minimum monthly wages, the GDP per capita, and the level of Economic Growth (GDP, annual variation in %) I conclude that migration flows from the countries of the Former Union to Turkey will continue, because female migrants seek a better standard of living and quality of life in Turkey and try to find a way of bettering their lives and those of their future children through marriage, employment or education in Turkey with the intention of staying there permanently.

Exploring political circumstances in the countries of the Former Soviet Union since their independence

The Soviet Union officially ceased to exist on 31 December 1991, and from that date the development of the 15 independent countries of the Former Soviet Union started.

During the period of the establishment of independence in these countries of the Former Soviet Union, from 1991 to 2016, numerous social upheavals, collapses, wars and revolutions have taken place.

In Armenia and Azerbaijan, the Nagorno-Karabakh War took place from 20 February 1988 to 12 May 1994. This conflict continues in 2016. [26]

---

[26] Nagorno-Karabakh is a "landlocked mountainous region of Nagorno-Karabakh is the subject of an unresolved dispute between Azerbaijan, in which it lies, and its ethnic Armenian majority, backed by neighbouring Armenia. In 1988, towards the end of Soviet rule, Azerbaijani troops and Armenian secessionists began a bloody war which left the de facto independent state in the hands of ethnic Armenians when a truce was signed in

Two Wars have taken place in the Russian Federation in the conflict between the Russian Federation and the Chechen Republic of Ichkeria. The First Chechen War was from 11 December 1994 to 31 August 1996, and the Second Chechen War was from 26 August 1999 to May 2000. Chechnya is "The southern Russian republic of Chechnya has long been a boiling point for conflict with Moscow in the restive North Caucasus. After a decade of unsuccessfully fighting for independence, the autonomous region is now firmly under the control of its Russian-appointed leader although separatist groups continue low-level guerrilla attacks."[27]

In Moldova the Transnistria War in 1992 took place from 2 March to 21 July 1992, and stalemate in this territory continues today. Trans-Dniester[28], a "separatist region, a narrow strip of land between the Dniester River and the Ukrainian border, proclaimed independence from Moldova in 1990, and is considered one of the post-Soviet space's "frozen conflicts". The international community does not recognise its self-declared statehood, and the territory, which remains in a tense stand-off with Moldova, is often portrayed as a hotbed of crime. In September 2006 referendum, unrecognised by Moldova and the international community, the region reasserted its demand for independence and also backed a plan eventually to join Russia. In the post World War II carve-up of the region, Moscow created Moldova's forerunner, the Moldavian Soviet Socialist Republic, from two disparate elements: the mainly Russian-speaking Dniester region, formerly an autonomous part of Ukraine, and the neighbouring region of Bessarabia, which had been part of Romania from 1918-1940. But in the Soviet Union's dying days, alarm grew in the Dniester region over growing Moldovan nationalism and the possible reunification of Moldova with Romania. A 1989 law which made Moldovan an official language added to the tension and Trans-Dniester proclaimed its secession in September 1990. The breakaway territory's paramilitary forces took over Moldovan public

---

1994. Negotiations have so far failed to produce a permanent peace agreement, and the dispute remains one of post-Soviet Europe's "frozen conflicts." The conflict has roots dating back well over a century into competition between Christian Armenian and Muslim Turkic and Persian influences. Populated for centuries by Christian Armenian and Turkic Azeris, Karabakh became part of the Russian empire in the 19th century. During the fighting, in which between 20,000 and 30,000 people are estimated to have lost their lives, the ethnic Armenians gained control of the region." See: BBC. 2016. "Nagorno-Karabakh profile." Accessed 25 May 2016. http://www.bbc.com/news/ world-europe-18270325.

[27] Accessed 25 May 2016. http://www.bbc.com/news/ world-europe.
[28] BBC. 2016. "Trans-Dniester profile." Accessed 25 May 2016. http://www.bbc.com/news/world-europe-18284837.

institutions in the area in 1991. Fighting intensified, culminating in a battle on the right bank of the Dniester in June 1992. Up to 700 people were killed in the conflict. A ceasefire was signed in July 1992, and a 10-km demilitarised security zone was established."

In Georgia the Revolution of Roses took place in November 2003, and the Russo-Georgian War happened in August 2008. During this War Georgia lost control of parts of Abkhazia and the former South Ossetian region. The Rose revolution[29] took place "in November 2003… Not one person was injured, not a drop of blood was spilled. Tens of thousands of demonstrators took to the streets to protest against the flawed results of a parliamentary election. The demonstrators demanded the resignation of a man who had ruled Georgia for more than 30 years in total. At that point, student demonstrators decided to give red roses to the soldiers. Many soldiers laid down their guns."

Two Revolutions have happened in Ukraine since independence. The Orange Revolution happened in 2004 from 22 November 2004 to 8 December, and the Revolution of Dignity happened in 2014 from 30 November 2013 to 23 February. On 27 February 2014 the occupation of Crimea by the Russian Federation took place and started the undeclared war of the Russian Federation against Ukraine in the Donbas region. This war also continues today. The two Ukrainian revolutions[30] were described as: "Ukrainians are back on the streets nine years after the Orange Revolution. In 2004-2005 mass protests have lasted for two months - the Orange Revolution - helped bring to power pro-Western President. In 2013-2014 mass protests have lasted for three months - the Revolution of Dignity - the biggest since the Orange Revolution. The mass demonstrations were triggered by the government's decision not to sign a wide-ranging association agreement with the European Union, because of pressure from Russia."

Due to all these wars, revolutions and conflicts in the territories of the countries of the Former Soviet Union, hundreds of thousands of people have fled the occupied areas and areas of military conflict and, because of this, numerous immigrants, refugees and asylum seekers came and continue to come to Turkey in search of a better life. They can count on some support in the host country because Turkey signed the 1951

---

[29] BBC. 2005. "How the Rose revolution happened." Accessed 25 May 2016. http://news.bbc.co.uk/2/hi/4532539.stm.

[30] BBC. 2013. "Ukraine's two different revolutions." Accessed 25 May 2016. http://www.bbc.com/news/world-europe-25210230.

Refugee Convention 30 March 1962 and its 1967 Protocol 31 July 1968[31] (United Nations High Commissioner for Refugees 2016).

According to Expat Guide Turkey, "the new Law on Foreigners and International Protection has been voted on the session of Turkish National Assembly on 04 April 2013. The new Law No.6458 on Foreigners and International Protection has been published in Government's Newspaper on 11 April 2013 No.28615" (Expat Guide Turkey 2013): "The Law on Foreigners and International Protection will make substantial changes in the Turkish asylum system, as well as it will outlaw the existing Law No.5683 Related to Residence and Travels of Foreigners. The new law will be mainly a Turkish asylum law and it will be treated as Turkish foreigners' code. New law specifies entry rules to Turkey, visa regulations and residence permit applications as well as it identifies the rules and principles regarding deportation and international protection. The Law on the Foreigners and International Protection also establishes the General Directorate of Migration Management under the Ministry of Interior. The following points are the major features of the new law about the residence permits. Following foreigners will be exempted from residence permit requirements: (i) foreigners who own a "certificate of stateless person"; (ii) officers of diplomatic and consular missions; (iii) those family members of the officers of diplomatic and consular missions (approval from the Ministry of Foreign Affairs is needed); (iv) officers of International Organizations, whose employment status has been determined by international agreements; (v) foreigners who are being exempted from the residence permit requirements by international agreements in which Turkey takes part; (vi) foreigners within the scope of article 28 of the Law No.5901 on Turkish Citizenship; (vii) foreigners who own a "Certificate of International Protection Applicant" or a "Refugee Certificate" granted in accordance with articles 69/7, 76/1 and 83/1 of the Law on Foreigners and International Protection."

Therefore, according to the Law of Turkey No.6458 of Foreigners and International Protection, the Article 30, [32] foreigners can obtain in Turkey several types of residence permits (Law of Turkey No.6458): "... foreigners can obtain in Turkey the following residence permit types:

---

[31]UNHCR - United Nations High Commissioner for Refugees - States Parties to the 1951 Convention and its 1967 Protocol. Accessed May, 2016. http://www.unhcr.org/3b73b0d63.html.

[32] The Turkish Parliament, Turkey. 2013. Law No. 6458 on 2013 of Foreigners and International Protection, 4 April 2013. Accessed May 8. http://www.refworld.org/docid/5167fbb20.html.

⊃ short-term residence permit;

⊃ family residence permit;

⊃ student residence permit;

⊃ long-term residence permit;

⊃ humanitarian residence permit;

⊃ victim of human trafficking residence permit."

Thus, due to the undeclared war in Ukraine, approximately 172,000 Ukrainians have applied for asylum in neighboring countries, according to the United Nations High Commissioner for Refugees (2015). Turkey was among the possible countries for Ukrainian asylum seekers: "The growing humanitarian needs in Ukraine require an urgent response. As of mid-September, more than 275,000 people had been displaced in Ukraine. Some 172,000 people had applied for asylum in neighboring countries in Europe, including more than 168,000 people in the Russian Federation."

During the period of my scholarship in Turkey I met refugees from the countries of the Former Soviet Union, Azerbaijan and Ukraine, in particular from Crimea and the occupied part of the Donbas region. These refugees had escaped from their homelands and are currently staying in Turkey as wives or brides of Turkish men thanks to family residence permits and tourist visas. Some of them have children from a former marriage in their native country and have brought those children with them to Turkey.

According to field research conducted in Turkey, I can identify some groups of refugees from the countries of the Former Soviet Union in Turkey:

⊃ The first group of refugees are families, who came to Turkey due to Wars in their countries of origin. Some of these families consist of several generations. The younger generations of refugees have already married in Turkey (for example, families of refugees from Azerbaijan who are living currently in Antalya and Istanbul);

⊃ The second group of refugees are single young women, who come to Turkey due to the unstable political situations in their countries of origin. They try to study, work or marry in Turkey (for example, young women from Crimea, Crimean Tatars who are living currently in the host country);

⊃ The third group of refugees are divorced women with or without children from previous marriages, who come to Turkey to marry (for example, women from Crimea and Donbas, who already are married in Turkey);

⊃ The fourth group of refugees are relatives of women who already live or work in the host country due to marriage or work permits. These relatives can be parents, sisters, brothers or adult children of the women (for example, women from Crimea and Donbas, who are married in Turkey).

International Agreements

International Agreements exist between some of the countries of the Former Soviet Union and Turkey and these can facilitate the integration of migrants and refugees, helping them to gain the status of workers into their host country.

According to data of the International Labor Organization (ILO), International social security agreements exist between Turkey and two of the countries of the Former Soviet Union, Georgia and Azerbaijan, and with a third country of the Former Soviet Union, Uzbekistan, a bilateral Agreement has been prepared, but not yet signed.

An International social security agreement between Turkey and Georgia "Agreement between Turkey and Georgia on Social Security" was signed on 11 December 1998 at Izmir, Turkey[33] (International Labor Organization 1998).

This international social security Agreement provides for the status of workers employed in both countries and for diplomatic staff. There are also agreements concerning medical assistance, maternity, disability, old age and unemployment benefits, and medical examinations.

A second international social security agreement exists between Turkey and Azerbaijan, the second of the countries of the Former Soviet Union, "Agreement between the Government of the Republic of Turkey and the Government of Azerbaijan on Social Security,"[34] signed on 17 July 1998 in Ankara, the capital of Turkey (International Labor Organization 1998).

---

[33] International Labour Organization (ILO). 1998. "Agreement between Turkey and Georgia on Social Security." Signed at Izmir on 11 December 1998. Resmi Gazete, 2003-11-12, No.25287, pp. 57-69. Accessed 10 May 2016. http://www.ilo.org/dyn/natlex/natlex4.detail?p_lang=en&p_isn=65891&p_country=TUR &p_count=781&p_classification=23.01&p_classcount=71.

[34] Ibid.

The bilateral Agreement between Turkey and the third country from the countries of the Former Soviet Union, Uzbekistan, has been not signed, only prepared in 1998.

These Agreements are very important for citizens of Georgia and Azerbaijan who work officially in Turkey because they allow citizens of Georgia and Azerbaijan to receive medical assistance, maternity, disability, old age and unemployment benefits, and medical examinations, but these agreements only cover citizens of these two countries out of all the 15 countries of the Former Soviet Union.

Unstable political and socio-economic circumstances in the countries of the Former Soviet Union

During the period of my scholarship in Turkey, I visited many different events where I could meet women from the countries of the Former Soviet Union. During my research, I used a qualitative field research method and a quantitative research method that is commonly employed in survey research, the structured interview. During the structured interviews, I asked women about their desire to obtain Turkish citizenship. Some of them told me that with Turkish citizenship they feel themselves more secure and comfortable than with citizenship of their native countries.

In my opinion, citizens of the countries of the Former Soviet Union, primarily women, would like to obtain dual citizenship in Turkey not only due to socio-economic reasons in their countries of origin and much better socio-economic situation in their host country, but also because of unstable political situations in their countries of origin.

In general, according to the structured interviews, 38% of women from the countries of the Former Soviet Union have obtained dual citizenship in Turkey, their host country (see Table 2.8).

According to data from my research, women from the three Baltic countries, Latvia, Lithuania and Estonia did not obtain dual citizenships because the socio-economic and political situations in their countries of origin remain stable. At the same time, women from Russia, Ukraine and the other countries of the Former Soviet Union try en masse to obtain dual citizenship in Turkey.

This is how some of them commented on their desires and their reasons to obtain dual citizenship in the host country:

Alla, 41 years old (10 years in Turkey): "For women with the Turkish citizenship it is easier to find a job in the host country, even if not in their own professions. Citizenship also provides guaranteed retirement benefits, and, of course, free and quality health services":

Anna, 35 years old (8 years in Turkey): "Women with Turkish citizenship have all rights of citizens of the country with all benefits from this dual citizenship";

Olga, 39 years old (15 years in Turkey): "Women with Turkish citizenship have a free choice of employment in any profession without permits and renewals";

Inna, 40 years old (10 years in Turkey): "Obtaining Turkish citizenship eliminates the need for a residence permit which involves an expensive and complicated procedure";

Lidia, 42 years old (9 years in Turkey): "The main benefit for women from the Turkish citizenship is employment without the need for a work permit and it gives women with a Turkish passport the right to vote.";

Table 2.8. Exploring the desire of women, who are citizens of the countries of the Former Soviet Union, to obtain a dual Turkish citizenship. (Number of women, citizens of the countries who participated in the structured interviews is 100%)

Countries	Number of women, citizens of the countries who obtained a dual Turkish citizenship (%)
Armenia	40
Azerbaijan	71
Belarus	40
Estonia	0
Georgia	22
Kazakhstan	46
Kyrgyzstan	36
Latvia	0
Lithuania	0
Moldova	45
Russia	42
Tajikistan	0
Turkmenistan	18
Ukraine	33
Uzbekistan	57
Total	38

According to *Cultural Law - International, Comparative, and Indigenous* (Nafziger et al., 2014), through a constitutional amendment of 5 December 1934 to the Constitution of the Republic of Turkey

(Turkish: Turkiye Cumhuriyeti Anayasası), "women obtained equal political rights with men".

Currently according to Chapter Four of the Constitution of the Republic of Turkey, Part II "Right to vote, to be elected and to engage in political activity," Article 67 (p. 29) (As amended on May 17, 1987; Act No. 3361, and on July 23, 1995; Act No. 4121) (International Labor Organization, 1995): "All Turkish citizens over eighteen years of age shall have the right to vote in elections and to take part in referenda."

Ekaterina, 50 years old (15 years in Turkey): "With Turkish citizenship women receive protection from the Turkish state";

Lidia, 42 years old (9 years in Turkey): "Citizenship of Turkey can give women bonuses and social guarantees in the host country."

Therefore, the majority of the women try to obtain Turkish citizenship for some bonuses and benefits in the host country. However, in the majority of the countries of the Former Soviet Union dual citizenship is forbidden.

I conclude that women from the countries of the Former Soviet Union try to obtain dual citizenship in Turkey because dual citizenship is allowed in Turkey and can give these women some bonuses and benefits, even if dual citizenship is not allowed in their countries of origin.

The main benefits that women would like to obtain dual citizenship are:

⊃   The right to vote in the host country;

⊃   Opportunities for legal jobs without any permits;

⊃   Retirement payments in future in Turkey;

⊃   Access to quality health services;

⊃   Entitlement to study at Turkish universities without charge;

⊃   Protection by Turkish Law in all situations in the host country including difficult situations;

⊃   Feeling themselves more comfortable in any situations in the host country.

Unstable political and socio-economic situations in the countries of the Former Soviet Union are reasons why women from the Former USSR would like to obtain Turkish citizenship.

The biggest percentage of women who have dual citizenship are women from Russia and Ukraine and this was 42% and 33% of all interviewed women from these countries in the framework of my research in Turkey.

Female migrants try to obtain dual citizenship in the host country even if dual citizenship is not allowed in the majority of their home countries of the Former Soviet Union.

I conclude that unstable political and socio-economic situations in the countries of the Former Soviet Union lead to female migration, and female migration flows only increase because the easiest way for women to solve their financial and other problems is a successful marriage with a foreigner, in particular with a Turkish man because currently Turkey has a very high level of socio-economic development and social security inside of the country. Therefore, women from the countries of the Former Soviet Union countries often try to marry Turkish men.

Post-Soviet political transformations, social changes in the countries of the Former USSR and its impact on female migration to Turkey

All of the countries of the Former Soviet Union, during the Post-Soviet period of independence, have passed through revolutions, wars, social upheavals, and collapses and in some of the countries this continues. The best situations were in the three Baltic countries, Estonia, Latvia and Lithuania because these countries, during the period of the Post-Soviet independence, became members of the European Union and have accepted the Euro as their national currencies. Therefore, standards of living and quality of life for residents of these countries are much better than for residents of other countries of the Former Soviet Union.

Three countries of the Former Soviet Union, Georgia, Ukraine and Moldova, have also declared their wish to join to the European Union in future. The Ukrainian nation particularly has paid a very high price for this desire because hundreds of Ukrainians were killed during the Revolution of Dignity or Euromaidan from the period of November 2013 to February 2014 in the capital of Ukraine, the city Kyiv.

Some political transformation and social changes also occurred in other countries of the Former Soviet Union, and the changes will be analyzed in this chapter.

Burke has analyzed political and social changes of the countries of the Former Soviet Union in the article "Post-Soviet world: what you need to know about the 15 states" (Burke, 2014).

This is what this author has written about political and social changes in Armenia in the Post-Soviet period of its history: "Armenia is the poorest country in the Caucasus, with roughly a third of the population living at or below the poverty line. The country's post-Soviet history has been defined by two diplomatic disputes with its neighbours. Domestically, Armenia has experienced bouts of political turbulence. With the domestic economy in the doldrums, hundreds of thousands of Armenians are abroad as migrant labourers, and their remittances are vital to the Armenian economy" (Burke, 2014).

Corruption has also had a strong and significant impact on political and social changes in the countries of the Former Soviet Union. According to the corruption perception index in 2015 made by the international organization Transparency International,[35] (Transparency International 2015), Armenia was under No.95 overall in the Corruption Perception Index ranking in 2015 and in this ranking the country was between two countries of the Former Soviet Union - between Georgia at No.48 and Moldova at No.103 (see Table 2.9).

Table 2.9. - Ranking of the Corruption Perception Index in 2015 thanks to data Transparency International

Corruption Perception Index (No. of each country)	Countries
154	Turkmenistan
153	Uzbekistan
136	Tajikistan
130	Ukraine
123	Kazakhstan
123	Kyrgyzstan
119	Russian Federation
119	Azerbaijan
107	Belarus
103	Moldova
95	Armenia
48	Georgia
40	Latvia
32	Lithuania
23	Estonia

[35] Transparency International. 2015. "Corruption perception index 2015." Accessed 20 May 2016. https://www.transparency.org/cpi2015/.

In the Corruption Perception Index, a lower position in the ranking means these countries are freer from corruption, and a higher position indicates a higher level of corruption in countries all over the world.

According to Burke on political and social changes in the countries of the Former Soviet Union, in particular Azerbaijan, in the article "Post-Soviet world: what you need to know about the 15 states" (Burke, 2014) he has written about current economic situation in Azerbaijan: "The post-Soviet era started disastrously with defeat in a war against neighboring Armenia. Azerbaijan's fortunes improved with the signing of an energy development deal in 1994 with a consortium of major oil companies. A pipeline to transport Azerbaijani energy from the Caspian basin to the west via Turkey began operating in 2006, generating billions in revenue annually for the government" (Burke, 2014).

According to the ranking of the Organization Transparency International, Azerbaijan was No.119 overall in 2015 and was between two countries of the Former Soviet Union with the same and similar Corruption Perception Index in 2015 - between Belarus at No.107 and the Russian Federation with the same No.119.

Burke has analyzed political and social changes of the countries of the Former Soviet Union in his article including Belarus, and in his opinion there is a close relationship between this country and Russia during the period of independence from the USSR: "Belarus is widely regarded as Europe's last dictatorship. Belarus has close ties with Russia, and the countries have signed a series of agreements to allow greater cooperation, although there have been periodic hiccups, including several Moscow-imposed cuts in natural gas supplies because of unpaid debts. Belarus is a charter member of a Russia-led customs union, which the Kremlin hopes to develop into an alternative EU for former Soviet states. The watchdog group Freedom House rates Belarus as "not free", and gives the country the worst grade possible when it comes to political rights" (Burke, 2014).

In the ranking of the Corruption Perception Index in 2015 Belarus was No.107 and was between two countries of the Former Soviet Union with the same and similar ranking in 2015 - between Azerbaijan at No.119 and Moldova at No.103.

As noted, Estonia, together with Latvia and Lithuania, has the best situation in political transformations and social changes because currently Estonia, Latvia and Lithuania are members of the European Union and have accepted the Euro as their national currencies: "Estonia is the smallest, least corrupt and most prosperous of all the former Soviet republics. The Baltic state rushed to embrace a market system after the

1991 Soviet collapse, and its economy is now powered by vibrant telecoms and electronics industries. The 2008 global financial crisis hit the country hard, sending unemployment spiraling. But stringent austerity measures quickly got the economy back on track. Estonia joined the EU and Nato in 2004, and, thanks to the quick recovery, entered the eurozone in 2011. After gaining independence, Lithuania looked westward, joining the EU and Nato in 2004. After the collapse of the USSR, Latvia underwent a dramatic transformation by rapidly turning west, joining the EU and Nato in 2004 and the eurozone in 2014. Latvia was the EU member hardest hit by the 2008 financial crisis, with unemployment topping 20% at one point. Years of austerity saw the country achieve one of the EU's most successful financial bounce-backs, yet unemployment remains stubbornly high, spurring many young Latvians to move abroad" (Burke, 2014).

Due to these positive changes in the three Baltic countries, Estonia was at No.23 according to a Corruption Perception Index Score in 2015 and became the country with the lowest level of corruption among the countries of the Former Soviet Union. Lithuania was at No.32 of the Corruption Perception Index Score in 2015, and Latvia was at No.40 in the ranking.

As noted about Georgia, this country would like to join to the European Union in future, and therefore the country is on the way to reforms and positive social changes: "Georgia has had a turbulent post-Soviet experience, to put it mildly, beset by separatist conflicts in two territories, Abkhazia and South Ossetia, and riven by a civil war that left the centre of the capital, Tbilisi, in ruins. Pervasive corruption and mismanagement fostered political and economic instability until 2003, before the Rose revolution. Currently Georgia completed negotiations on its initial EU association agreement in 2013, placing the country on a firmer path towards full membership" (Burke, 2014).

In the ranking of the Corruption Perception Index in 2015 Georgia was at No.48 and was between two countries of the Former Soviet Union, behind Latvia at No.40 and above Armenia at No.95 in this ranking.

Kazakhstan is a country of the Former Soviet Union with large oil reserves on its territory and due to this its economy has good prospects for development: "Thanks to energy exports, Kazakhstan is central Asia's most prosperous state, with annual economic growth averaging about 10% for much of the first decade of the new millennium. Kazakhstan has the second largest oil reserves among the former Soviet republics after Russia, and its oil exports are expected to soar as its huge

Kashagan oil field, in the Caspian Sea, develops. In recent years, the gap between rich and poor in Kazakhstan has widened, heightening social tensions" (Burke, 2014).

In the ranking of the Corruption Perception Index in 2015 Kazakhstan was at No.123 above Ukraine with its No.130 and the same as Kyrgyzstan at No.123.

Concerning Kyrgyzstan, there is a high level of poverty, unemployment and corruption, and the minimum monthly wage is the lowest among the countries of the Former Soviet Union: "This mountainous central Asian state enjoyed relative stability during the early years of independence. High unemployment and widespread poverty mean Kyrgyzstan is a major source of migrant laborers" (Burke, 2014).

In the ranking of the Corruption Perception Index in 2015 Kyrgyzstan was at No.123 between the Russian Federation at No.119 and Kazakhstan with the same ranking.

Concerning Moldova, there is a high level of migration flows from the country due to poverty, unemployment and corruption, and in 2013 the country declared its direction to the future EU membership: "In late 2013, Moldovan authorities entered an agreement with the EU, placing the country on a path towards full membership. According to IMF data, Moldova is among Europe's poorest countries. There were repeated bouts of internal political and economic turmoil during the late 1990s and early 2000s, though the situation has stabilized in recent years" (Burke, 2014).

In the ranking of the Corruption Perception Index in 2015 Moldova was at No.103 and was between two countries of the Former Soviet Union - between Armenia at No.95 and Belarus at No.107 in the Corruption Perception Index ranking (Transparency International, 2015).

The Russian Federation is the biggest country among the countries of the Former Soviet Union and tries to retain power over the other countries of the Former Soviet Union: "The post-Soviet period has had a Dickensian flavour for Russia - it has been the worst of times, followed by better times. From 1991 to 1999 was an era marked by economic dysfunction, lawlessness, rampant corruption and a ruinous war in the southern territory of Chechnya. Although corruption remained prevalent, a mood of prosperity returned - at least to Moscow and St Petersburg. Analysts suspect that one of chief goals of the current president is the expansion of Russian influence in other formerly Soviet republics under the guise of an economic union, and the Moscow-dominated Eurasian Union would function as an alternative EU" (Burke, 2014).

In the ranking of the Corruption Perception Index in 2015 Russia was at No.119 and between Azerbaijan at the same No.119 and Kyrgyzstan at No.123.

Concerning Tajikistan, this country has a high level of unemployment, poverty, mismanagement and corruption and due to this a large number of Tajik citizens work outside of their country of origin: "Tajikistan is the poorest of all formerly Soviet republics, according to the UNDP's human development index. Shortly after the Soviet collapse in 1991, it descended into a civil war that pitted government forces dominated by the former Communist party elite against a broad coalition that included Islamists and pro-western elements. The domestic economy is characterized by widespread corruption, mismanagement and unemployment, and many areas of the country endure blackouts on a regular basis. More than a million Tajiks, or about an eighth of the population, are believed to be in Russia as guest workers. Remittances from these migrant labourers are estimated to account for 52% of GDP, according to World Bank data" (Burke, 2014).

In the ranking of the Corruption Perception Index in 2015 Tajikistan was at No.136 in the overall Corruption Perception Index rankings in 2015 and was between two countries of the Former Soviet Union - between Ukraine at No.130 and Uzbekistan at No.153.

Turkmenistan has on its territory large oil reserves and these natural resources may enable the raising of the level of development of the country, particularly in the area of social changes for citizens of this country: "Turkmenistan is among the most corrupt and repressive countries on earth, according to watchdogs. It also possesses the fourth-largest proven reserves of natural gas in the world. Economically, gas exports enable the government to maintain its tight grip on power. By 2013, Turkmenistan was China's largest foreign supplier of natural gas" (Burke, 2014).

In the ranking of the Corruption Perception Index in 2015 Turkmenistan was at No.154 in the overall Corruption Perception Index rankings and was the country with the highest level of corruption among all the countries of the Former Soviet Union.

Ukraine has also had a high level of corruption in recent years, and this was one of reasons for the Revolution of Dignity in late of 2013 - start of 2014 in Ukraine. Ukraine tries to make positive changes and reforms in the country, and, as was noted, would like to join to the

European Union in due course: "For some, the protests that erupted in November 2013 may have come as a surprise. For many others, it was only ever a matter of time before tensions boiled over in a country that spent the post-Soviet era zigzagging between east and west. Political and economic uncertainty persisted. In late 2013 the former president backed away from signing an association agreement with the EU, prompting large-scale protests, which came together in the Euromaidan movement. A pro-western coalition took power. In late February, Russian troops, in unmarked uniforms, moved into the Crimean Peninsula to support local separatists and in March, Russia annexed Crimea" (Burke, 2014).

In the ranking of the Corruption Perception Index in 2015 Ukraine was at No.130 in the overall Corruption Perception Index rankings in 2015 and was between two countries of the Former Soviet Union - between Tajikistan at No.136 and Kazakhstan at No.123.

In the case of Uzbekistan, the country has large gas reserves, but the level of corruption is so high that any development of positive changes for citizens of the country is too slow: "Uzbekistan is central Asia's most populous state and strives to assert itself as a regional power. Economically, tight state controls have fostered stagnation and popular resentment while hindering foreign investment. The country's primary exports are natural gas and cotton" (Burke, 2014).

In the ranking of the Corruption Perception Index, Uzbekistan was at No.153 and was the second country after Turkmenistan with the highest level of corruption in 2015 among the countries of the Former Soviet Union.

So, according to the Corruption Perception Index in 2015, the lowest index of corruption among the countries of the Former Soviet Union with an index under No.23 was Estonia, and the highest index of corruption among the countries of the Former Soviet Union was Turkmenistan at No.154 in the Corruption Perception Index in 2015.

Hence I conclude that Post-Soviet political transformations and social changes in the countries of the Former USSR have very significant impact on female migration to Turkey. Thi is because from the countries of the Former Soviet Union countries where political transformations and social changes are successful and effective, the percentage of female migrants is minimal. From other countries of the Former Soviet Union where poverty, unemployment and corruption are high, female migrants flows only increase and female migrants try to solve all, or the majority, of their problems through marriage with Turkish men, because currently Turkey has a very high level of socio-economic development and social security.

Therefore, women from the countries of the Former Soviet Union countries migrate in ever greater numbers to marry Turkish men.

Some women came to Turkey as refugees due to wars in their countries of origin. Some groups of refugees from the countries of the Former Soviet Union come to Turkey for other reasons. So, the first group of refugees are families, who came to Turkey due to wars in their countries of origin, and some of these families consist of several generations. The younger generations of refugees have already married in Turkey (for example, families of refugees from Azerbaijan who are living currently in Antalya and Istanbul). The second groups of refugees are single young women, who come to Turkey due to the unstable political situation in their countries of origin. They try to study, work or marry in Turkey (for example, young women from Crimea, Crimean Tatars who are living currently in the host country). The third groups of refugees are divorced women with or without children from previous marriages, who come to Turkey to marry (for example, women from Crimea and Donbas, who already are married in Turkey). The fourth groups of refugees are relatives of women who already live or work in Turkey due to marriage or work permits. These relatives can be parents, sisters, brothers or adult children of the women (for example, women from Crimea and Donbas, who are married in Turkey).

In order to understand the desire of women to marry Turkish men, it was very important to analyze political and socio-economic situations including indexes of corruption in the countries of origin of the women, using the data from the International organization Transparency International in 2015. Thus, according to the Corruption Perception Index in 2015, the lowest index of corruption among the countries of the Former Soviet Union with an index was Estonia at No.23, and the highest index of corruption among the countries of the Former Soviet Union was Turkmenistan because this country was at No.154. The Corruption Perception Index is important index because it helps to explain increases in female migrant flows from some of the countries of the Former Soviet Union to Turkey.

CHAPTER 3

CHALLENGES FACED BY MIGRANT WOMEN IN TURKEY

Language barrier

In 2012 the Ukrainian TV channel 1+1 presented a program "Change a woman"[36] about the situation of one female migrant in Turkey, who is married to a Turkish man. The couple have lived together for six years in Turkey but the woman did not speak Turkish and the man did not speak Ukrainian, Russian or English. Therefore, for this couple the language barrier was one of their main problems and it prevented them from living in harmony because they could not understand each other.

Unfortunately, the language barrier is one of the most common problems for female migrants from the countries of the Former Soviet Union in the host country.

Women from the countries of the Former USSR may meet Turkish men during tourist visits and seasonal work in Turkey or in their own home countries through Turkish companies working in different areas of the economy. Women can also meet men through the Internet, through marriage agencies, or through friends and acquaintances. Many married couples encounter problems because of the language barrier. During my field research many women cited this problem as one of the most common problems of female migrants in the host country. Women from counties with Turkic languages, for example, Azerbaijani, Kazakh, Kyrgyz, Gagauz, Uyghur, Tatar, Crimean Tatar, Turkmen, Uzbek, or Sakha are able to learn the Turkish language quickly and easily.

It is possible to classify Turkic languages by branch (Encyclopædia Britannica 2016): "Turkic languages -group of closely related languages that form a subfamily of the Altaic languages. The Turkic languages show close similarities to each other in phonology, morphology, and syntax, though Chuvash, Khalaj, and Sakha differ considerably from the rest. The Turkic languages may be classified, using linguistic, historical, and geographic criteria, into a southwestern (SW), a northwestern (NW), a southeastern (SE), and a northeastern (NE) branch. The southwestern, or Oghuz, branch comprises three groups. The West Oghuz group

---

[36] TV Channel 1+1. 2012. The program "Change a woman." Accessed 17 May 2016. https://www.youtube.com/watch?v=eteiA0t84YA.

(SWw) consists of Turkish; Azerbaijani; and Gagauz. The East Oghuz group (SWe) consists of Turkmen. The southwestern, or Oghuz, branch comprises three groups. The West Oghuz group (SWw) consists of Turkish; Azerbaijani; and Gagauz. The East Oghuz group (SWe) consists of Turkmen. A southern group (SWs) is formed by Afshar and related dialects in Iran and Afghanistan. The northwestern branch comprises three groups. The South Kipchak group (NWs) consists of Kazakh, and Kyrgyz. The North Kipchak group (NWn) consists of Tatar, Bashkir, and West Siberian dialects. The West Kipchak group (NWw) today consists of Crimean Tatar. The southeastern, or Uighur-Chagatai, branch comprises two groups. The western group (SEw) consists of Uzbek. The northeastern, or Siberian, branch comprises two groups. The North Siberian group (NEn) consists of Sakha and Dolgan." [37]

Hence, the Turkish language belongs to the West Oghuz group, Azerbaijani to the West Oghuz group, Kazakh to the South Kipchak group, Kyrgyz to the South Kipchak group, Gagauz to the West Oghuz group, Uyghur to the eastern group of the southeastern or Uighur-Chagatai branch, Tatar to the North Kipchak group, Crimean Tatar to the West Kipchak group, Turkmen to the East Oghuz group, Uzbek to the western group of the southeastern or Uighur-Chagatai branch, and Sakha to the northeastern or Siberian branch.

According to the findings of my field research in Turkey it is possible to analyze the levels of knowledge of the Turkish language (Native, Advanced, Intermediate or Elementary) of women from the different countries of the Former Soviet Union in Turkey (Table 3.1).

For computations I have defined all women of each country as 100%, in this case a percentage of women of each country will be parts out of 100%.

I have calculated the percentage of all responses of women in the project by their level of knowledge of the Turkish language (Native, Advanced, Intermediate or Elementary), and the number of all responses from women about their level of knowledge of the Turkish language of each of the countries I have marked as 100%.

Out of all women who participated in the structured interviews in the framework of the scientific project, 14% of women have a native level in the Turkish language; 37% have an advanced level; 33% have an

[37] Encyclopædia Britannica. 2016. "Turkic languages." Accessed 26 May 2016. http://www.britannica.com/topic/Turkic-languages.

intermediate level; and 16% have an elementary level of knowledge of the Turkish language.

Therefore, the majority of Armenian women have advanced level of knowledge of the Turkish language (60%). The majority of Azerbaijani women have a very high level of knowledge of the Turkish language - like a native (43%) and a high level of knowledge of the Turkish language - advanced (43%).

The majority of Belarusian women have an intermediate level of knowledge of the Turkish language (60%). Estonian women have native and intermediate levels of knowledge of the Turkish language. The percentage of Georgian women, due to their level of knowledge of the Turkish language, is almost proportional - 22% of women have a native, advanced and elementary level, and 33% of them have intermediate level.

Table 3.1. Level of knowledge of the Turkish language (in %)

Women from the countries	Level of knowledge of the Turkish language (parts out of 100%)			
	Native	Advanced	Intermediate	Elementary
Armenia	20	60	20	0
Azerbaijan	43	43	14	0
Belarus	8	24	60	8
Estonia	50	0	50	0
Georgia	22	22	33	22
Kazakhstan	23	46	15	15
Kyrgyzstan	27	27	9	36
Latvia	25	50	0	25
Lithuania	17	17	33	33
Moldova	35	50	10	5
Russia	11	42	31	17
Tajikistan	0	0	100	0
Turkmenistan	0	55	45	0
Ukraine	9	31	39	22
Uzbekistan	14	29	57	0
Total women (100%)	14	37	33	16

Kazakhstani women 46% have a high level of knowledge of the Turkish language - advanced. Kyrgyzstani women 36% have an elementary level of knowledge of the Turkish language. Half of Latvian women have a high level of knowledge of the Turkish language - advanced (50%).

17% of Lithuanian women have native level of knowledge of the Turkish language; 17% have advanced level; 33% have intermediate level; and 33% have an elementary level. Half of Moldovan women have a high level of knowledge of the Turkish language - advanced (50%). 42% of women from Russia have an advanced level of knowledge of the Turkish language. All the women from Tajikistan have intermediate level. The majority of Turkmen women have an advanced level of knowledge of the Turkish language (55%).

9% of women from Ukraine have a native level of knowledge of the Turkish language; 31% have advanced level; 39% have intermediate level; and 22% have an elementary level. The majority of Uzbek women 57% have an intermediate level of knowledge of the Turkish language.

In fairness, it should be noted that each of these women have been in Turkey for different periods of time which is a very important factor in learning a language. Some of them have lived there for just a few weeks or months and others have been there for 10 and more years.

Thus, the most common problem of female migrants from the countries of the Former Soviet Union in the host country is the language barrier.

Violence and abuse

Second most common problem of female migrants from the countries of the Former Soviet Union in Turkey is violence and abuse in their families and in Turkish society. During structured interviews, I asked them about any discrimination or harassment in the host country and about any discrimination or harassment within their Turkish families.

From the narratives of interviewed women, I conclude that not all of them have stable and positive situations in their families in the areas of discrimination, violence or abuse. According to the results of structured interviews, only a small percentage of women experienced discrimination, abuse or violence, but I can say with confidence that during field research I heard of numerous cases of violence and abuse in families and there are a few reasons why women do not want to talk of these subjects. They are sometimes afraid to talk about it; they do not want to talk about problems in their families, or they do not realize that what they are experiencing is discrimination, abuse or unreasonable violence.

Table 3.2 presents the results of structured interviews about discrimination, abuse or violence in Turkish families or Turkish society towards women from the countries of the Former Soviet Union.

According to the findings of the field research, 20% of interviewed women from Armenia felt discrimination or harassment in the host society.

7% of Azerbaijani women felt discrimination or harassment in the host society, and 14% among them felt discrimination or harassment within their Turkish families.

20% of Belarusian women felt discrimination or harassment in the host society, and 8% of them felt discrimination or harassment within their Turkish families (4% of women did not respond).

100% of Estonian, 75% of Latvian and 33% of Lithuanian women felt discrimination or harassment in the host society, and 50% of Estonian and 25% of Latvian women felt discrimination or harassment within their Turkish families.

22% of Georgian, 15% of Kazakhstani and 9% of Kyrgyz women felt discrimination or harassment in the host society, and 8% of Kazakhstani women felt discrimination or harassment within their Turkish families.

40% of Moldovan and 19% of Russian women felt discrimination or harassment in the host society, and 35% of Moldovan and 9% of Russian women felt discrimination or harassment within their Turkish families.

Women from Tajikistan did not reply about discrimination or harassment in Turkey or in their Turkish families.

9% of Turkmen, 21% of Ukrainian and 57% of Uzbek women felt discrimination or harassment in the host society, and 9% of Turkmen, 16% of Ukrainian and 71% of Uzbek women felt discrimination or harassment within their Turkish families.

We can conclude that domestic violence, discrimination and abuse against women from the Former Soviet Union in Turkey are not rare occurrences in their families. In brief, in this research I have found that domestic violence and abuse is present for 14% of Azerbaijani women; 8% of Belarusian and Kazakhstani women; 50% of Estonian and 25% of Latvian women; 35% of Moldovan women; 9% of Russian and Turkmen women; 16% of Ukrainian women and 71% of Uzbek women in their families in the host country.

With the aim of protecting the family and preventing violence against women, the Turkish Parliament adopted the Law on Prevention of Domestic Violence (The Law to Protect Family and Prevent Violence

Against Women, Law No. 6284 from 8 March 2012, The Grand National Assembly of Turkey) on 8 March 2012.[38]

However for various reasons, only a small percentage of women are ready to go to police for protection, which means that they are afraid and alone in the host country with their problems.

Table 3.2. Discrimination, abuse or violence in Turkish families or by Turkish society towards women from the former Soviet Union countries, in %

Women from the countries	Have you experienced any discrimination or harassment in the host society? (parts out of 100%)		Have you experienced any discrimination or harassment within your Turkish family? (parts out of 100%)	
	Yes	No	Yes	No
Armenia	20	80	0	100
Azerbaijan	7	93	14	86
Belarus	20	80	8	88
Estonia	100	0	50	50
Georgia	22	78	0	100
Kazakhstan	15	85	8	91
Kyrgyzstan	9	81	0	100
Latvia	75	25	25	75
Lithuania	33	67	0	100
Moldova	40	60	35	65
Russia	19	81	9	91
Tajikistan	0	100	0	100
Turkmenistan	9	91	9	91
Ukraine	21	79	16	84
Uzbekistan	57	43	71	29

According to Sevinclidir (2015) the situation with domestic violence is pessimistic in Turkey: "Turkey made no progress in reducing domestic violence between 2008 and 2014, according to the Domestic Violence Against Women Report 2014.The report said almost 40% of women in Turkey had been physically abused at least once in their lifetime. One in 10 had been also subjected to sexual violence by their partner, it added" (Sevinclidir, 2015).

---

[38] Parliament of Turkey. 2012. "The Law to Protect Family and Prevent Violence Against Women." Law No.6284 from 8 March 2012. Accessed 8 June 2016. http://www.lawsturkey.com/law/law-to-protect-family-and-prevent-violence -against-woman-6284.

The second most common problem of female migrants from the countries of the Former Soviet Union in the host country is domestic violence, discrimination and abuse.

Unemployment

The third most common problem for female migrants from the countries of the Former Soviet Union in the host country is employment for women. Some women work in the host country, some of them even work in their own professions, some of them work freelance, and some work illegally or on a temporary basis. However, the problem of self-employment for women from the countries of the Former Soviet Union is very topical.

In general, the problem of self-employment is related to the reputation of female migrants, who came en masse to Turkey twenty years ago and have worked there as prostitutes. Many Turks have the preconception that all female migrants from the Former USSR are 'Natasha', which is the common name that was used for all women of easy virtue from the countries of the Former Soviet Union. This name has been in common usage since that time.

Because of this, for women from the countries of the Former Soviet Union it is very difficult to find a good and official job in Turkey. Husbands of female migrants may forbid them to work.

Tables 3.3 and 3.4 present the results of structured interviews about employment problems of women from the countries of the Former Soviet Union in the host country and their desire to work in Turkey (parts out of 100%).

As before, I have defined all responses of interviewed women from each country as 100%, in this case a percentage of responses in all tables of this chapter will be parts out of 100%.

In the responses of Georgian, Kazakhstani and Kyrgyz women, those employed in Turkey were 100% of all interviewed, Georgian, 62% of Kazakhstani and 73% of Kyrgyz women, and 33% of Georgian, 23% of Kazakhstani and 18% of Kyrgyz women work in their professions.

Overall 80% Armenian women who participated in the interviews are employed and 20% of these work in their professions.

64% of Azerbaijani women are employed in general, and 29% of them work in their professions.

In responses from Belarusian women, 40% of them are employed (4% of them work temporarily and 8% of them work illegally) in general, and 12% of employed women work in their professions (8% of women did not respond).

Table 3.3. Employment problems of women from the countries of the Former Soviet Union living in Turkey, and about their desire to work in Turkey, in %

Women from the countries	Employment in the host country (parts out of 100%)		Do you work in your profession? (parts out of 100%)	
	Yes	No	Yes	No
Armenia	80	20	20	80
Azerbaijan	64	36	29	71
Belarus	40	60	12	80
Estonia	100	0	100	0
Georgia	100	0	33	67
Kazakhstan	62	38	23	77
Kyrgyzstan	73	27	18	82
Latvia	50	50	25	75
Lithuania	67	33	17	83
Moldova	60	40	15	85
Russia	38	62	18	82
Tajikistan	100	0	100	0
Turkmenistan	82	18	27	73
Ukraine	44	56	16	84
Uzbekistan	71	29	14	86

In their responses, 100% of all interviewed Estonians, 50% of Latvians and 67% of Lithuanians are employed in Turkey, and 100% of all interviewed Estonians, 25% of Latvians and 17% of Lithuanians work in their professions.

In the responses from Moldovan and Russian women, 60% Moldovans and 38% of Russians are employed in Turkey, and 15% of Moldovans and 18% of Russians work in their professions.

The Russian women from Tajikistan, who are not Tajik women, when interviewed all confirmed that they are employed in Turkey and work in their professions.

In the responses of Turkmen, Ukrainian and Uzbek women, 82% of all interviewed Turkmen, 44% of Ukrainian and 71% of Uzbek women are employed in Turkey, and 27% of Turkmen, 16% of Ukrainian and 14% of Uzbek women work in their professions.

Table 3.4 presents the results of structured interviews about the opportunities and the desire to work of women from the countries of the Former Soviet Union in Turkey.

Table 3.4. Opportunities and desire to work in Turkey, in %

Women from the countries	Do you have the opportunity to work? (parts out of 100%)		Do you have a desire to work? (parts out of 100%)	
	Yes	No	Yes	No
Armenia	40	60	80	20
Azerbaijan	86	14	71	29
Belarus	80	20	84	16
Estonia	100	0	100	0
Georgia	100	0	100	0
Kazakhstan	92	8	85	15
Kyrgyzstan	100	0	91	9
Latvia	75	25	100	0
Lithuania	50	50	83	17
Moldova	95	5	95	5
Russia	78	22	84	16
Tajikistan	100	0	100	0
Turkmenistan	82	18	64	36
Ukraine	81	19	84	16
Uzbekistan	86	14	100	0

In the responses of Armenian women, 40% of them have opportunities to work in Turkey in general and legally in particular; and 80% of them have a desire to work.

86% of Azerbaijani women have opportunities to work and 71% of them have a desire to work.

80% of Belarusian women have opportunities to work in general, and 84% of them have a desire to work.

100% of Estonian, 75% of Latvian and 50% of Lithuanian women have opportunities to work, and 100% of Estonian, 100% of Latvian and 83% of Lithuanian women have a desire to work.

100% of Georgian, 92% of Kazakhstani and 100% of Kyrgyz women have opportunities to work, and 100% of Georgian, 85% of Kazakhstani and 91% of Kyrgyz women have a desire to work.

95% of Moldovan and 78% of Russian women have opportunities to work, and 95% of Moldovan and 84% of Russian women have a desire to work.

100% of women from Tajikistan have opportunities to work, and 100% of the women have a desire to work.

82% of Turkmen, 81% of Ukrainian and 86% of Uzbek women have opportunities to work, and 64% of Turkmen, 84% of Ukrainian and 100% of Uzbek women have a desire to work.

The third most common problem for female migrants from the countries of the Former Soviet Union in the host country is unemployment of women.

Access to quality health services and retirement pension provision

The fourth most common problem of female migrants from the countries of the Former Soviet Union in Turkey is access to quality health services and retirement pension provision.

Table 3.5 presents the results of structured interviews about access to quality health services and retirement pension provision for women from the countries of the Former Soviet Union in the host country.

Table 3.5. Access to quality health services and retirement pension provision, in %

Women from the countries	Do you have access to quality health services? (parts out of 100%)		Will you have the right to retirement pensions? (parts out of 100%)	
	Yes	No	Yes	No
Armenia	20	80	20	80
Azerbaijan	93	7	100	0
Belarus	96	4	52	36
Estonia	100	0	50	50
Georgia	22	78	22	78
Kazakhstan	92	8	69	31
Kyrgyzstan	73	27	45	55
Latvia	100	0	75	25
Lithuania	100	0	50	50
Moldova	80	20	50	50
Russia	90	10	57	43
Tajikistan	100	0	50	50
Turkmenistan	73	27	27	73
Ukraine	85	15	54	46
Uzbekistan	57	43	57	43

20% of Armenian women have access to quality health services, and the same percentage of women have the right to retirement pension payments.

93% of Azerbaijani women have access to quality health services, and 100% of interviewed women have the right to retirement pension payments in the host country.

96% of all interviewed Belarusian women have access to quality health services, and 52% of them have the right to retirement pension payments in Turkey (12% of women did not respond).

100% of Estonian, Latvian and Lithuanian women have access to quality health services, and 50% of interviewed Estonian, 75% of Latvian and 50% of Lithuanian women have the right to retirement pension payments.

22% of Georgian, 92% of Kazakhstani and 73% of Kyrgyz women have access to quality health services, and 22% of Georgian, 69% of Kazakhstani and 45% of Kyrgyz women have the right to retirement pension payments.

80% of Moldovan and 90% of Russian women have access to quality health services, and 50% of Moldovan and 57% of Russian women have right to retirement pension payments.

100% of women from Tajikistan have access to quality health services, and 50% of the women have the right to retirement pension payments.

73% of Turkmen, 85% of Ukrainian and 57% of Uzbek women have access to quality health services, and 27% of Turkmen, 54% of Ukrainian and 57% of Uzbek women have the right to retirement pension payments.

So, the fourth most common problem for female migrants from the countries of the Former Soviet Union in the host country is access to quality health services and retirement pension provision.

20% of Armenian women have access to quality health services, 93% of Azerbaijani women, 96% of all interviewed Belarusian women, 22% of Georgian, 92% of Kazakhstani, 73% of Kyrgyz women, 80% of Moldovan and 90% of Russian, 73% of Turkmen, 85% of Ukrainian, and 57% of Uzbek women.

According to the Turkish Social Security and Universal Health Insurance Law No.5510, which is also known as the Turkish Social Security Law, some women from the countries of the Former Soviet Union in Turkey, who are wives or widows of Turkish men, are entitled to receive social insurance or some part of the pension of their husbands (Amended on 17 April 2008 - 5754/21st Art.).[39]

If women cannot count on their husbands pensions and are not covered by the Turkish Social Security and Universal Health Insurance Law of Turkey, or do not have Turkish husbands, they can take out private pension plans with Turkish banks. This was established in October 2001 after the enactment of the Turkish Law No.4632 - Private Pension Plans Savings and Investment System, but only a small percent of women from the countries of the Former Soviet Union can pay for their private pension plans every month for long enough to benefit.[40]

Gender inequality

The problem of gender inequality is one of the common problems of women, not only foreign women, but also Turkish women. In cases of women from the countries of the Former Soviet Union they are faced with a large number of restrictions from their husbands or their relatives. Not all women can accept these restrictions.

Turkey is a secular and a religious country at the same time and if women are married to non-religious Turkish men, they can feel themselves freer in their families and in Turkish society and very often they can work or study in the host country.

However, if women are married to religious Turkish men, very often they have converted to Islam and so cannot work because, in opinion of their husbands, their sole duty is motherhood.

According to the World Economic Forum's Global Gender Gap Index 2014 (GGG Index), published by the Forum, Turkey is No.125 out of 140 countries of the world in 2004 (World Economic Forum 2014).

In this Global Gender Gap Index 2014 the lower ranking means that these countries have less gender inequality and the higher ranking indicates a higher level of gender inequality in countries of the world.

---

[39] The Law of Turkey. 2006. "Turkish Social Security and Universal Health Insurance Law: 5510" (The date of enactment of the Law was 31 May 2006, and the date of entry into force was 01 October 2008). Accessed 8 June 2016. http://turkishlaborlaw.com/turkish-social-security-law-no-5510.

[40] The Law of Turkey. 2001. "The Law on Individual Pension Savings and Investment System No.4632" (Date of Ratification 28 March 2001; Date of Publication 7 April 2001). Accessed 8 June 2016. http://www.sigortadenetim .org/mevzuat/ngilizce-mevzuat/118.html.

For countries of the Former Soviet Union, two out of 15 countries of the Former USSR were in this Global Gender Gap Index 2014, specifically Turkmenistan and Uzbekistan (Table 3.6).

In the Global Gender Gap Index 2014, Armenia was at No.103 and was the country with the highest level among all the countries of the Former Soviet Union.

Table 3.6. Global Gender Gap Index 2014 (GGG Index) (World Economic Forum 2014)

GGG Index (No. of each country)	Countries
103	Armenia
102	Tajikistan
94	Azerbaijan
85	Georgia
75	Russian Federation
67	Kyrgyzstan
62	Estonia
56	Ukraine
44	Lithuania
43	Kazakhstan
32	Belarus
25	Moldova
15	Latvia

Azerbaijan was No.94 overall in 2014 and was between two countries of the Former Soviet Union with similar Global Gender Gap Indexes - between Georgia at No.85 and Tajikistan at No.102.

In the ranking of the Global Gender Gap Index 2014 Belarus was No.32 and was between two countries of the Former Soviet Union with similar indexes - between Kazakhstan at No.43 and Moldova at No.25.

In the ranking of the Global Gender Gap Index 2014 Estonia was at No.62, Lithuania was at No.44, and Latvia was at No.15 and became the country with the lowest level of gender inequality in 2014 among the countries of the Former Soviet Union.

In the ranking of the Global Gender Gap Index 2014 Georgia was at No.85 and was between two countries of the Former Soviet Union, behind the Russian Federation at No.75, and above Azerbaijan at No.94.

In the ranking of the GGG Index in 2014 Kazakhstan was at No.43, above Lithuania with its No.44 and behind Belarus at No.32.

In the ranking of the Index in 2014 Kyrgyzstan was at No.67 between the Russian Federation at No.75 and Estonia at No.62.

Moldova was at No.25 and was between two countries of the Former Soviet Union - between Latvia at No.15 and Belarus at No.32.

Russia was at No.75 and this ranking was between two countries of the Former Soviet Union - between Georgia at the No.85 and Kyrgyzstan at No.67.

Tajikistan was at No.102 in the overall Index rankings in 2014 and was between two countries of the Former Soviet Union - between Armenia at No.103 and Azerbaijan at No.94.

Ukraine was at No.56, and this ranking was between two countries of the Former Soviet Union - between Lithuania at No.44, and Estonia at No.62.

Let us return to Turkey where gender inequality is too high, causing problems for many women from the countries of the Former Soviet Union in their families and in society in general.

So, the fifth most common problem for female migrants from the countries of the Former Soviet Union is the problem of gender inequality in the host country especially for women from the countries of the Former Soviet Union because they often have little opportunity to protect themselves from domestic violence, abuse or harassment.

Hence, I conclude that women from the countries of the Former Soviet Union have many problems in the host country. In my opinion, the first most common problem for female migrants from the countries of the Former Soviet Union is the language barrier with husbands, their relatives, and other people. This is a big problem for women because they cannot communicate with other people and cannot work even if they have the desire and the opportunity.

The second most common problem for female migrants from the countries of the Former Soviet Union is domestic violence, discrimination and abuse within the family. In my opinion, people who were born in different countries with different cultures and have a language barrier cannot understand each other completely, and so cannot create happy relationships. In these cases, domestic violence, discrimination and abuse can occur. Turkey has passed laws to protect the family and prevent violence against women; the Law No.6284 on Prevention of Domestic Violence has adopted the Parliament of Turkey 8 March 2012, but not all women are ready to go to police to ask for protection. They are afraid and alone in the host country with their problems.

The third most common problem for female migrants from the countries of the Former Soviet Union in the host country is unemployment of women. According to the results of my structured interviews, 80% Armenian women who participated in interviews are employed in the host country, 64% of Azerbaijani women, 40% of Belarusian women (4% of them work temporarily and 8% of them work illegally), 100% of all interviewed Estonian women, 50% of Latvian women, 67% of Lithuanian women, 100% of all interviewed Georgian women, 62% of Kazakhstani women, 73% of Kyrgyz women, 60% Moldovan women, 38% of Russian women, 82% of Turkmen women, 44% of Ukrainian women, and 71% of Uzbek women are employed. Only 20% of Armenian women, 29% of Azerbaijani women, 12% of Belarusian women, 25% of Latvian women, 17% of Lithuanian women, 33% of Georgian women, 23% of Kazakhstani women, 18% of Kyrgyz women, 15% of Moldovan women, 18% of Russian women, 27% of Turkmen, 16% of Ukrainian and 14% of Uzbek women work in their professions. In my opinion this problem is further complicated by reputation of women from the countries of the Former Soviet Union in Turkey of being women of easy virtue or 'Natasha'. Not all employers are ready to offer them vacancies and these women are often more subject to sexual harassment than women of other nationalities. I think that the reputation of 'Natasha', which has been so entrenched in Turkey for 20 years towards women from the countries of the Former Soviet Union, still causes suffering to many women from the Former USSR.

The fourth most common problem for female migrants from the countries of the Former Soviet Union in Turkey is access to quality health services and retirement pension provision. The lowest percentage of women who have access to quality health services in Turkey among interviewed women are women from Armenia - 20% of Armenian women; from Georgia - 22% of Georgian women; and from Uzbekistan - 57% of Uzbek women. These women do not have access to quality health services. According to the Turkish Social Security and Universal Health Insurance Law No.5510, which is also known as the Turkish Social Security Law (The date of enactment of the Law was 31 May 2006 and the date of entry into force was 01 October 2008), some women from the countries of the Former Soviet Union in Turkey, who are wives or widows of Turkish men, are entitled to receive social insurance or a part of their husbands' pensions. Under Article 34 of the Law No.5510, female migrants who are wives or widows of Turkish men, and their children can be protected by this Law (Amended on 17 April 2008 - 5754/21st Art.). If women cannot count on their husbands pensions and are not covered by the Turkish Social Security and

Universal Health Insurance Law of Turkey, or do not have Turkish husbands, they can take out private pension plans with Turkish banks. This was established in October 2001 after the enactment of the Turkish Law No.4632 - Private Pension Plans Savings and Investment System, but only a small percent of women from the countries of the Former Soviet Union can pay for their private pension plans every month for long enough to benefit.

The fifth most common problem for female migrants from the countries of the Former Soviet Union in Turkey is the problem of gender inequality. According to data from the World Economic Forum and its Global Gender Gap Index 2014 (GGG Index), published by the Forum, Turkey was No. 125 out of 140 countries of the world and was behind all countries of the Former USSR that appeared in this GGG Index in 2014 excluding Turkmenistan and Uzbekistan. Women from the Former USSR, who would like to marry Turkish men, always need to be aware of the traditionally dominant roles of Turkish men in families and society and decide before marriage if they are able to accept a role that will be secondary to that of their husband.

CHAPTER 4

HUMAN CAPITAL: POTENTIAL FOR TURKEY

The term 'Human Capital' appeared in the 1960s in USA and it means talents, knowledge, skills and generation of ideas of people for scientific and technical progress in the world. Founders of the theory of Human Capital were American scientists, both recipients of the Nobel Prize in Economic Sciences, Theodore William Schultz and Gary Stanley Becker. "... the economist Theodore William Schultz invented the term "human capital" in the 1960s to reflect the value of human capacities. He believed human capital was like any other type of capital; it could be invested in through education, training and enhanced benefits that lead to an improvement in the quality and level of production"[41].

According to Becker (2016), author of the book "A Theoretical and Empirical Analysis, with Special Reference to Education", he is "a pioneer of applying economic analysis to human behavior in such areas as discrimination, marriage, family relations, and education": "Human Capital is Becker's classic study of how investment in an individual's education and training is similar to business investments in equipment. Becker is a pioneer of applying economic analysis to human behaviour in such areas as discrimination, marriage, family relations, and education. Becker's research on human capital was considered by the Nobel committee to be his most noteworthy contribution to economics" (Becker, 2016).

According to Theodore W. Schultz, investment in human capital is direct expenditures on education, health, and migration: "Much of what we call consumption constitutes investment in human capital. Direct expenditures on education, health, and internal migration to take advantage of better job opportunities are clear examples" (Schultz 1961).

Migration is also defined as one way for individuals and families to adjust to changing job opportunities, among five major categories of activities that improve human capabilities (Schultz, 1961): "Activities that improve human capabilities five major categories: (1) health facilities and services, broadly conceived to include all expenditures that affect the life expectancy, strength and stamina, and the vigor and vitality of a people; (2) On-the job training, including old-style

---

[41] Investopedia. 2016. "Human Capital." Accessed 8 May 2016. http://www.investopedia.com/terms/h/humancapital.asp.

apprenticeship organized by firms; (3) formally organized education at elementary, secondary and higher levels; (4) study programs for adults that are not organized by firms, including extension programs in agriculture; (5) Migration of individuals and families to adjust to changing job opportunities" (Schultz, 1961).

I have studied issues of human capital in my thesis "Human Capital Management in the Retail Food Industry" (Koshulko, 2008), and in my book titled "Human capital in Ukraine: how we do not value what we have" (Koshulko, 2012).

Human capital of women who come to Turkey for various reasons is a very valuable commodity for any country, both for the development of society and the economy. Women who have university degrees have valuable human capital and they need to continue to develop their careers and their human capital. The results of my research show that a large percentage of women from the countries of the Former USSR have Ph.D. degrees and universities degrees (Table 4.1).

Table 4.1. Educational level of female respondents from the countries of the Former Soviet Union, in %

Women from the countries	Your educational level (in %)			
	Ph.D. Degree	Graduate degree	College Degree	High School Degree
Armenia	0	100	0	0
Azerbaijan	14	72	7	7
Belarus	0	76	20	4
Estonia	0	100	0	0
Georgia	0	22	22	56
Kazakhstan	8	62	15	15
Kyrgyzstan	0	55	27	18
Latvia	0	100	0	0
Lithuania	17	83	0	0
Moldova	5	50	35	10
Russia	4	76	13	7
Tajikistan	0	100	0	0
Turkmenistan	10	36	36	18
Ukraine	5	65	12	18
Uzbekistan	0	57	29	14

Of course, the level of education of women differs depending on their country of origin. For example, the educational level of interviewed women from Estonia or Latvia is generally higher than the educational level of women from other countries.

The highest educational level is that of women from Lithuania (17% of women with Ph.D. degree); then Azerbaijan (14% of women with Ph.D. degree); Turkmenistan (10% of women with Ph.D. degree); Kazakhstan (8% of women with Ph.D. degree); Ukraine (5% of women with Ph.D. degree); Moldova (5% of women with Ph.D. degree); and Russia (4% of women with Ph.D. degree). In these cases I can say with confidence that the educational level of these women is a very high.

Regarding graduate degrees, thanks to the results of the research in Turkey, it is possible to say that 100% of interviewed women from Armenia have a graduate degree; 72% of Azerbaijani women have a graduate degree; 76% of Belarusian women; 100% of Estonian, 100% of Latvian and 83% of Lithuanian women; 22% of Georgian, 62% of Kazakhstani and 55% of Kyrgyz women; 50% of Moldovan and 76% of Russian women; 100% of women from Tajikistan; 36% of Turkmen, 65% of Ukrainian and 57% of Uzbek women.

I conclude that the educational level of women from the Former Soviet Union in Turkey is a very high. 100% of interviewed women from Armenia, Estonia, Latvia, and Tajikistan have a Graduate degree. The majority of women from Azerbaijan; Belarus; Lithuania; Kazakhstan; Kyrgyzstan; Russia; Ukraine; Uzbekistan have a Graduate degree as well as half the women from Moldova.

How can they use their educational level in the host country? As shown only 20% of Armenian women work in their own professions, 29% of Azerbaijani women work in their own professions, 12% of Belarusian women, 25% of Latvian women, 17% of Lithuanian women, 33% of Georgian women, 23% of Kazakhstani women, 18% of Kyrgyz women, 15% of Moldovan women, 18% of Russian women, 27% of Turkmen, 16% of Ukrainian and 14% of Uzbek women work in their own professions in Turkey.

Human capital consists of basic and professional human capital and in cases when women cannot work in their professions in the host country and cannot use their professional human capital, they can use their basic human capital working in other or unskilled professions.

I met numerous women who work in jobs other than their own professions in Turkey, from translators and teachers of Russian to cleaners and sales people. Of course due to life situations many women have changed their professions in Turkey. I met a lot of women who did not work in their own professions due to various circumstances in their lives. Therefore, their human capital did not develop in their own professions and they suffered Brain Waste and Human Capital depreciation.

What is human capital depreciation? What causes human capital to depreciate? According to data from Investopedia, 'human capital deprecation is directly caused by interruptions in a work career, such as periods of unemployment' (Investopedia, 2016):

"A relative or absolute decline in human capital is most commonly associated with unemployment, the inability to keep up with technological innovations, physical injury or mental decomposition. Economists and business analysts have studied the impact of wage rate growth or decline following different life events, such as earning a degree or returning to work following an extended hiatus, with mixed and controversial results. In economic theory, specialization increases an individual's marginal revenue product (MRP) by making the worker more efficient at producing a good or service. If specialization is achieved through repetition, training and focus, then it would be easy to assume that the cessation of repetition, training and focus would cause MRP to decrease. Workers who are unemployed for long periods of time are unlikely to maintain their previous levels of specialization or may find that their past skills are less in-demand than before. The positive correlation between specialization and wage rate has led many economists to claim that human capital deprecation is directly caused by interruptions in a work career, such as periods of unemployment. Some have suggested that the unequal burdens placed on women during marriage, such as housekeeping and child rearing, are directly responsible for gender wage gap - a theory called the marital asymmetry hypothesis - because the opportunity cost of being married is vocational specialization".

I have studied the human capital depreciation of immigrants in an earlier article titled "Exploring of the Human Capital Depreciation of Ukrainian Labor Migrants Abroad: Results of a Survey," and I concluded that when skilled workers, for whatever reasons, are forced to move abroad and to work as unskilled workers, there is a very big problem of Brain Waste for all sides (Koshulko, 2015): "... when skilled workers, for whatever reasons, are forced to move abroad and to work as unskilled workers, there is a very big problem of Brain Waste for all sides, for skilled workers, who were professionals in the past, for their country of origin and for their host countries too. Very often these skilled workers, professionals in the past, when they return to their country of origin, find that they cannot work in their previous professions, which is a worse situation for them. Of course, during a period of labor migration abroad, labor migrants, professionals in the past, can develop new skills and knowledge, but, unfortunately, labor migrants often perform unskilled work abroad. In my opinion, the biggest problems for skilled workers seeking work as professionals in host countries are language barriers, problems with confirmation of diplomas in host countries, lack of competitive knowledge and skills on international labor markets" (Koshulko, 2015).

In Turkey, there exists the problem of recognition of academic diplomas of foreigners in general and those of women from the Former USSR in particular. In the host country this procedure of recognition of academic diplomas of foreigners can be done at the Council of Higher Education (CoHE) (in Turkish: Yuksekogretim Kurulu Baskanlıgı) in the capital of Turkey Ankara, but not all women can complete this procedure of recognition of academic diplomas for a number of reasons:

⊃ because the recognition of academic diplomas can take up to year or more;

⊃ because of the language barrier in cases where applicants need to pass tests or exams in the Turkish language;

⊃ because of lack of support from husbands and / or their relatives in this issue;

⊃ because of periods of maternity leave;

⊃ because of other issues.

Women can also take courses TOMER at the Turkish and Foreign Languages Research and Application Center of Ankara University or in its branches in Istanbul, Trabzon, Giresun, Samsun, Marmaris, Izmir, Bursa, Antalya and Alanya that can help them to improve their knowledge of Turkish and so gain recognition of their academic diplomas faster and more easily.

In cases where women do not try to get recognition of their diplomas in the host country and do not try to find a job in their own professions (always supposing their husbands allow them to do so), they can lose their human capital and professional knowledge and skills as time passes.

My previous research shows that for every 12 month period skilled immigrants will lose around 1.2% of their existing Human Capital (Koshulko, 2015) if they cannot continue to develop their human capital in the host country.

Opportunities and desires

During my research in Turkey, I asked women about their opportunities and their desires to continue their education or to get a higher education. From their replies I conclude that not all of them can study even if they have the desire to do so.

Table 4.2 shows the responses of women from all the countries of the Former Soviet Union. I have calculated the percentage of all responses of the women, and total responses of women from each of the countries I have marked as 100%.

Table 4.2. Opportunities to continue their education or to get a higher education and about their desire to do so, in %

Women from the countries	Do you have the opportunity to continue your education or to get a higher education? (parts out of 100%)		Do you have a desire to continue your education or get an education? (parts out of 100%)	
	Yes	No	Yes	No
Armenia	60	20	20	80
Azerbaijan	86	14	64	36
Belarus	56	40	72	28
Estonia	100	0	100	0
Georgia	11	89	11	89
Kazakhstan	46	54	46	54
Kyrgyzstan	64	36	36	64
Latvia	100	0	100	0
Lithuania	67	33	50	50
Moldova	60	40	75	25
Russia	66	34	61	39
Tajikistan	50	50	100	0
Turkmenistan	27	73	36	64
Ukraine	51	49	55	45
Uzbekistan	29	71	71	29

I conclude that 60% Armenian women have opportunities to continue their education or to get a higher education, but only 20% of them have the desire to do so (20% of Armenian women did not respond).

The responses of Azerbaijani women in Turkey show that - 86% of Azerbaijani women have opportunities to continue their education or to get a higher education and 64% of them have the desire to do so.

The responses of Belarusian women show that - 56% of Belarusian women have opportunities to continue their education or to get a higher education (4% of women did not respond), and 72% of them have the desire to do so.

The responses of Estonian, Latvian and Lithuanian women show that - 100% of all interviewed Estonian, 100% of Latvian and 67% of Lithuanian women have opportunities to continue their education or to get a higher education, and 100% of all interviewed Estonian, 100% of Latvian and 50% of Lithuanian women have the desire to do so.

The responses of Georgian, Kazakhstani and Kyrgyz women show that - 33% of Georgian, 54% of Kazakhstani and 91% of Kyrgyz women have opportunities to continue their education or to get a higher education, and 11% of Georgian, 46% of Kazakhstani and 64% of Kyrgyz women have the desire to do so.

The responses of Moldovan and Russian women show that - 60% of Moldovan and 66% of Russian women have opportunities to continue their education or to get a higher education, and 75% of Moldovan and 61% of Russian women have the desire to do so.

The responses of women from Tajikistan show that - 50% of women have opportunities to continue their education or to get a higher education, and 100% of them have the desire to do so.

The responses of Turkmen, Ukrainian and Uzbek women show that - 27% of Turkmen, 51% of Ukrainian and 29% of Uzbek women have opportunities to continue their education or to get a higher education, and 36% of Turkmen, 55% of Ukrainian and 71% of Uzbek women have the desire to do so.

Human capital consists of basic and professional human capital and, in cases when women cannot work in their own professions in the host country and cannot use their professional human capital, they are able to use their basic human capital and work in other or unskilled professions.

I met numerous women in Turkey who are in work that is different from their own professions, from translators and teachers of Russian to cleaners and sales people. In these cases, their professional human capital cannot develop and this constitutes Brain Waste, which after some time will become human capital depreciation of the professional skills and knowledge. These women will not be able to return to work in their professions nor will they be able to work in the more junior positions.

The majority of women, who come to Turkey for various reasons, would like to work, study, and develop their human capital in any areas of the economy. If they are in the situation where they cannot work in their professions, they try to gain new professional skills, to do unskilled jobs or to find other spheres of fulfillment for their human capital.

Some of these women cannot work and develop their Human Capital in the host country because their husbands forbid them do so, because of their belief that maternity is the only acceptable occupation for women in Turkey. In these cases, it is very difficult for women to gain fulfillment as professionals and holders of quality human capital. Should this situation change and they are able to return to their professions, they will encounter problems because their human capital has depreciated.

Periods of maternity leave also have a significant impact on human capital accumulation or depreciation of women in Turkey and in my research I interviewed many women who were on maternity leave. The responses of Azerbaijani women in Turkey show that 21% of them were on maternity capital leave, 8% of Belarusian the women, 8% of Kazakhstani women, 5% of Moldovan, 14% of Russian women, 9% of Turkmen and 13% of Ukrainian women were on maternity leave.

Returning to work after a period of maternity leave is also very difficult and impacts on their ability to continue developing their professional human capital.

CHAPTER 5

VARYING CAUSES AND OUTCOMES OF MOVEMENT FOR WOMEN

Differences among women who migrate are the very essence of this situation; differences in their reasons for migration and the causes and in their level of culture and education. This process is very personal because each of them views the process of migration differently. Some of them travel intending to marry and have children, which for them is enough. For other women the most important thing is their careers or their business in the new country.

There are also differences in the causes of female migration to Turkey from the countries of the Former Soviet Union. One group of women are escaping the poverty and unemployment in their own countries. A second group of women come to Turkey to escape the wars and revolutions in their countries of origin and a third group are escaping difficult relationships in families in their home countries.

There are also differences in the nationalities and ethnic groups of women from the countries of the Former Soviet Union. Participants of this project were women of 27 nationalities and ethnic groups from the 15 countries of the Former Soviet Union. Ten or 37% of these nationalities and ethnic groups belong to the Turkic people, and, in my opinion, female migrants who belong to the Turkic people, may adapt in Turkey more easily than women of other nationalities and ethnic groups who also migrate to Turkey.

The next difference is the religion of women from the Former USSR. Women from Azerbaijan, Kazakhstan, Kyrgyzstan, Turkmenistan and Uzbekistan have the same religion as Turkey and so they feel more comfortable in Turkish society than women from Armenia, Belarus, Estonia, Georgia, Latvia, Lithuania, Moldova, Russia, and Ukraine. Some of the women of some non-Muslim countries of the Former USSR convert to Islam for various reasons.

The next difference is unwillingness to convert to another religion. Some women feel able to convert to Islam and to so receive benefits from this situation in Turkish families and Turkish society. However, some women feel unable to convert in any situation. I have met women who have converted to Islam; I have met women who stay in their

Orthodox religion and I have also met women who become apostates after converted to Islam.

These differences are obstacles to be overcome by women wanting to migrate to Turkey. Some women study the Turkish language and culture at universities and take courses in Turkish with the aim of going to Turkey, staying officially and working as professionals. Other women go to Turkey to improve their lives in other ways.

The subjects of my research and my monograph are women who stay officially in Turkey with the intention of working, marrying or studying, but it is not possible to gather accurate data about other women from the countries of the Former Soviet Union who are in Turkey. They remain invisible in this country and work as prostitutes either willingly or unwillingly. It is not possible to know their histories and their tragedies because they are part of the criminal and illegal economy in the host country but they also count in the number of women from the countries of the Former USSR. There are differences in ability and willingness to perform such work among the women from the countries of the Former Soviet Union. For example, there is a district in the city of Antalya that is nicknamed 'Natasha' because everybody knows that prostitutes live there. So, there are differences between women in the areas of life style, behavior in the country of origin, the different types of lives they wish to lead in Turkey.

Similarities in the migration of women to Turkey from the different Former Soviet Union countries are in their desire to start a new life in Turkey. As noted, women come to Turkey for various reasons - to marry, to study, to found a business and for other reasons. In these cases, their former life has finished and they are starting an absolutely new page in the story of their life in their new country.

All of them pass through the stages of adaptation in the host country. According to data Kalervo Oberg in his book "Culture Shock: Adjustment to New Cultural Environments" (Oberg, 1960) all migrants go through distinct phases: Honeymoon, Crisis, Recovery, and Adjustment.

According to Irwin, "...culture shock is the depression and anxiety experienced by many people when they travel or move to a new social and cultural setting" (Irwin, 2007). Such culture shock is an experience shared by all women from the Former USSR in the host country and it is very important for women to receive support and help from their husbands and their relatives.

The next similarity among women is the necessity to accept some general rules in Islamic Sharia Law if they decide to marry Turkish men. In this case women from the countries of the Former Union who not Muslim need to accept the following rules of Islamic Sharia Law in Turkey:

- ⊃ Women need to accept the fact that children born from marriages with Muslim men will be considered Muslims;

- ⊃ Women need to accept that according to the rules of Islamic Sharia, male children must be circumcised, which is standard practice among Muslims;

- ⊃ Women need to know that in the event of divorce, or the death of the husband, Islamic Sharia decrees that in mixed marriages where the husband is Muslim and the wife is not, the wife will lose custody of the children;

- ⊃ Women need do accept that wives of Muslim men cannot travel with their children without the permission of their husbands;

- ⊃ Women need to know that in situation of inheritance, according to the general rule in Islamic Sharia, women inherit half the share of men who have the same degree of relation to the deceased (Sawma 2013).

These rules are taken seriously and all women need to accept this if they decide to marry Turkish men.

I have also identified the following three areas that may be affected by issues arising from migration of women to Turkey from the countries of the Former Soviet Union countries:

- ⊃ issues for female migrants in the host country;

- ⊃ issues for female migrants in their countries of origin after a period of time spent in another country (return migration);

- ⊃ issues for the countries of the Former Soviet Union affected by the flow of female emigrants.

Let us consider each of these issues that may arise for women due to their migration from the countries of the Former Soviet Union to Turkey:

Issues for female migrants in the host country may be manifested by different forms of discrimination in the host society. Piper and French (2011) have suggested that female migrants in a host country face dual discriminations because they are women and they are non-citizens there: "Indeed, gender-based inequalities, injustice, discrimination and outright violence continue to permeate all societies to a certain extent, in some form or another. Such outcomes are often brought to the surface through, or are the result of, the migrant experience which, for women, typically means dual discrimination on the basis of being female and a non-citizen or absent citizen. Yet migration may allow women to turn these negative outcomes around by gaining greater control of their lives, whether through escape from traditional gender roles, improved knowledge and awareness about their rights, or newfound financial independence. Whether they migrate between two societies with opposing or comparable human development situations, women may find that they are liberated simply by having taken on a new role because of the move" (Piper, 2011: 1-3).

Issue arising from female migration for women, if they are not happy with their husbands and / or their Turkish relatives, may be manifested by forms of alcoholism or other negative reactions if women cannot change their lives in Turkey or return to their home country. If they do not have opportunities and second chances in their lives, they may lose all motivation and become alcoholics, and unfortunately, I have seen such women in Turkey.

Issues from female migration arise not only for migrants themselves, but also for their children and grand children. Guveli and colleagues (2015) have written about Intergenerational consequences of migration with reference to socio-economic, family and cultural patterns of stability and change in Turkey and Europe as they emerge in the processes of migration. The results of scientific research show that the majority of women have children, and, of course, the positive or negative migration experience of their mothers will impact on their lives and will have some consequences. In my opinion there may be different types of consequences for women and their children.

The first type is when women have left their children in their countries of origin and come to Turkey to marry. Outcomes that may be attributed to this situation: complex relationships between mothers and children; malice; hatred; disrespect towards the mothers for life; jealousy of younger siblings arriving in the new marriages of mothers.

The second consequence may be when women take their children to the host country where they will meet new relatives and stepfathers. This situation may bring about, particularly for older children, complex relationships between mothers, children, stepfathers and their new Turkish relatives; difficulty adapting to a new environment and a new society; malice; hatred; disrespect to mothers; jealousy of younger siblings arriving in the new marriages of their mothers.

Female migrants returning to their countries of origin after staying away for whatever reasons may experience divorces, deportation or other consequences. These situations may be most complicated when women were forced to leave their children in the host country. I would like to share a few real case histories of women who came back to their country of origin from Turkey.

Olga, 45 years old. She was married to a Turkish man for 6 years. She has one son. She did not know the Turkish language, traditions or culture and so her husband's family did not accept her as a daughter-in-law. As a consequence of the bad attitude shown to her by her husband's relatives, she left Turkey even though her husband has twice sought a reconciliation because of their son. She came back to her country of origin 10 years ago. She has a diploma in teaching, but she works as a seller on a market because she lost her professional skills and knowledge (Brain Waste) and she cannot work as a teacher. This situation demonstrates Human capital depreciation as the woman cannot work in her profession of teacher. She was unhappy in Turkey and she has no desire ever to return there.

Inga, 42 years old. She was in Turkey for two months with her two children but she faced bad treatment from relatives of her Turkish man. Besides, when she came to Turkey he was still married, but in the process of divorce. When she decided to return to her country of origin he went with her with the aim of saving their relationship. She has a law degree, so when she came back, she opened a law office and she works in her profession. She did not continue her relationship with the Turkish man and he returned to his home country. In this case Brain Drain did not occur because the woman was in the host country for only two months. The woman continues to work in her profession in her country of origin. She had not been able to see any prospects for herself, her children and her career in Turkey and therefore decided to return to her country of origin.

So, both of these women had relationships with Turkish men. The women did not work in the host country and they both returned to their country of origin due to complicated relationships with relatives and parents of their men, who were unable to accept these women for various reasons, including the language barrier and differences in culture, traditions and values.

Female migration from the countries of the Former Soviet Union to Turkey has a negative impact on the countries of origin of the women because the majority of the countries of the Former Soviet Union have an ageing population and a negative population growth rate.

Thus, according to estimates of Index Mundi in 2014[42], population growth rate in Armenia was (-0.13%), in Azerbaijan 0.99%, in Belarus (-0.19%), in Estonia (-0.68%), in Georgia (-0.11%), in Kazakhstan (1.17%), in Kyrgyzstan (1.04%), in Latvia (-0.62%), in Lithuania (-0.29%), in Moldova (-1.02%), in Russia (-0.03%);, in Tajikistan (1.75%), in Turkmenistan (1.14%), in Ukraine (-0.64%); and in Uzbekistan (0.93%) (Table 5.1).

A ranking of the population growth rates according to estimates by Index Mundi for 2014 has been created and consists of two parts: a ranking of the countries of the Former Soviet Union of positive and negative rates in 2014 (Table 5.2).

In this ranking of the positive and negative population growth rates of the countries of the Former Soviet Union in 2014 the negative population growth rates means that in some countries there is depopulation or demographic collapse and the positive ranking indicates a growth in population and a surplus of births over deaths in some countries of the Former Soviet Union in 2014.

Thus, according to this ranking, demographic collapses in 2014 were in Moldova (a negative population growth rate was -1.02%); in Estonia (a negative population growth rate was -0.68%); in Ukraine (a negative population growth rate was -0.64%); in Latvia (a negative population growth rate was -0.62%); and in Lithuania (a negative population growth rate was -0.29%).

In other countries of the Former USSR with negative population growth rates, these rates were low, and these countries were Belarus (a negative population growth rate was -0.19%); Armenia (a negative population growth rate was -0.13%); Georgia (a negative population growth rate was -0.11%); and Russia (a negative population growth rate was -0.03%).

---

[42] Data was extracted from Index Mundi, (Accessed: 15/5/2016): http://www.indexmundi.com/ azerbaijan/population_growth_rate.html; http://www.indexmundi.com/belarus/ population_growth_rate.html; http://www.indexmundi.com/estonia/ population_ growth_rate.html; http://www.indexmundi.com/ georgia/population_growth_rate.html; http://www.indexmundi.com/kazakhstan/population_growth_rate.html; http://www.indexmundi.com/kyrgyzstan/ population_growth_rate.html; http:// www. indexmundi.com/ latvia/ population_growth_rate.html; http://www. indexmundi. com/lithuania/population _growth_rate.html; http://www.indexmundi. com /moldova/population_growth _rate.html; http://www. indexmundi. com/russia/ population_growth_rate.html; http://www.indexmundi. com/ tajikistan/ population_ growth_rate.html; http://www.indexmundi.com/ turkmenistan/population_ growth _rate.html; http://www.indexmundi.com/ukraine /population_growth_rate.html; http://www.indexmundi.com/uzbekistan/ population_growth_rate.html.

Table 5.1. Population growth rates of the countries of the Former Soviet Union in 2014 (Index Mundi) in %

Women from the countries:	Population growth rate of the countries
Armenia	-0.13%
Azerbaijan	0.99%
Belarus	-0.19%
Estonia	-0.68%
Georgia	-0.11%
Kazakhstan	1.17%
Kyrgyzstan	1.04%
Latvia	-0.62%
Lithuania	-0.29%
Moldova	-1.02%
Russia	-0.03%
Tajikistan	1.75%
Turkmenistan	1.14%
Ukraine	-0.64%
Uzbekistan	0.93%

In 2014, the positive population growth rates of the countries of the Former Soviet Union were in Uzbekistan (a positive population growth rate was 0.93%); Azerbaijan (a positive population growth rate was 0.99%); Kyrgyzstan (a positive population growth rate was 1.04%); Turkmenistan (a positive population growth rate was 1.14%); Kazakhstan (a positive population growth rate was 1.17%); and Tajikistan (a positive population growth rate was 1.75%).

The lowest of the negative population growth rates among the countries of the Former Soviet Union was -1.02% in Moldova in 2014 which means there is a demographic collapse in that country and the highest of the positive population growth rates among the countries of the Former Soviet Union was 1.75% in Tajikistan in 2014 which means a growth in population and a surplus of births over deaths in this country in 2014.

The estimates suggest a strong and significant effect of female migrant flows on countries of origin of women, i.e. the countries of the Former Soviet Union, because in the majority of the countries the population growth rates are negative.

One of reasons for these situations is female migration to Turkey. A significant percentage of women from these countries get married and have children abroad. Very often mothers also take children from their previous marriages to the host country in order to give them more and better prospects in life.

Table 5.2. Positive and negative population growth rates of the countries of the Former Soviet Union in 2014 (Index Mundi)

Countries of the Former USSR	Positive population growth rates in %	Countries of the Former USSR	Negative population growth rates in %
Uzbekistan	0.93%	Moldova	-1.02%
Azerbaijan	0.99%	Estonia	-0.68%
Kyrgyzstan	1.04%	Ukraine	-0.64%
Turkmenistan	1.14%	Latvia	-0.62%
Kazakhstan	1.17%	Lithuania	-0.29%
Tajikistan	1.75%	Belarus	-0.19%
		Armenia	-0.13%
		Georgia	-0.11%
		Russia	-0.03%

I conclude that differences in the migration of women are in the characters of female migrants, in their purposes and causes, in their level of culture and education; in events that have stimulated female migration to Turkey from the countries of the Former Soviet Union; in the nationalities and ethnic groups of women from the countries of the Former Soviet Union; in the religion of women from the Former USSR; in their willingness or otherwise to convert to another religion; in ways of achieving the desired goals; in the life styles of female migrants, in their behaviour in the country of origin, in their desires to build different lives in Turkey.

Similarities in the migration of women to Turkey from the different Former Soviet Union countries are seen in the desires of women to start a new life in Turkey; in stages of adaptation in the host country; and particularly in the necessity of accepting general rules in Islamic Sharia if women decide to marry Turkish men.

Consequences from migration of women to Turkey from the countries of the Former Soviet Union countries may arise for female migrants in the host country; for women returning to their countries of origin after failed migration and for the countries of origin of female migrants.

Consequences for female migrants in the host country may be manifested in various forms of discrimination in the host society; in forms of alcoholism or other negative reactions if the women cannot change their lives in the host country or return to their host countries; in the consequences for children and grand children of female migrants.

Consequences for female migrants returning to their countries of origin after being away may be due to various reasons, divorces, deportation etc. These situations may be most complicated when women were forced to leave their children in Turkey.

Consequences for the countries of the Former Soviet Union through female migrant flows to Turkey may appear as an increase in ageing and in the negative population growth rates in the majority of the countries of the Former Soviet Union.

The results of this research show that in 2014 demographic collapses and depopulation were in Moldova, Estonia, Ukraine, Latvia and Lithuania. The negative population growth rates were also in Belarus, Armenia, Georgia, and Russia. In 2014 the positive population growth rates of the countries of the Former Soviet Union were in Uzbekistan, Azerbaijan, Kyrgyzstan, Turkmenistan, Kazakhstan, and Tajikistan, and in these cases, the lowest of negative population growth rate was in Moldova in 2014, and the highest of the positive population growth rate was 1.75% in Tajikistan.

Therefore, the consequences of female migrant flows on the countries of the Former Soviet Union are not positive because in the majority of the countries the population growth rates are negative and one of reasons of these situations is female migration from the countries of origin to Turkey.

Types of organizations in Turkey that can help female migrants from the countries of the Former Soviet Union

In situations of divorce, division of property, custody of children, domestic violence and / or other difficult life situations for female migrants in Turkey they need professional help.

Female migrants experiencing such difficult situations may receive help in Turkey from some state and non-governmental organisations: from the Turkish police; from the Embassies and Consulates of their own countries of origin; from associations of their compatriots in Turkey and from the Centers of psychological and legal support to migrants.

For many different reasons, not all women are ready to go to police in Turkey because they may be there illegally and are afraid of deportation; women may be afraid of inciting retaliation by their husbands; they may not believe that police can solve their problems; they have language barriers and other reasons. In these cases some of most effective places to seek help and support are the Embassies and Consulates of their own countries in Ankara, Istanbul and some other cities of Turkey.

The first institutions that may help them are the diplomatic institutions of their countries of origin, the countries of the Former Soviet Union, with the exception of Armenia. Below are listed the names of diplomatic missions that may help female migrants experiencing difficulties in Turkey. Embassies of each of the countries of the Former Soviet Union, with the exception of Armenia, are situated in the capital of Turkey and Consulates are in Istanbul and other cities of Turkey:

Embassy of the Republic of Azerbaijan;

Embassy of the Republic of Belarus;

Estonian Embassy;

Embassy of Georgia;

Embassy of the Republic of Kazakhstan;

Embassy of the Kyrgyz Republic;

Embassy of Latvia;

Embassy of the Republic of Lithuania;

Embassy of the Republic of Moldova;

Embassy of the Russian Federation;

Embassy of the Republic of Tajikistan;

Embassy of Turkmenistan Republic;

Embassy of Ukraine;

Embassy of the Republic of Uzbekistan.

Some Associations (in Turkish: Dernek or Dernegi) of compatriots of the countries of the Former Soviet Union are to be found in Turkey and these institutions may support female migrants especially at the time of their first steps in Turkey. The Associations (Dernek or Dernegi) of the majority of the countries of the Former Soviet Union can be found in Istanbul.

Below are names of some Associations in Istanbul that can help immigrants from the countries of the Former Soviet Union with some of their problems such as the Association of the Armenians; the Association of the Azerbaijanis; the Association of the Georgians.

Certainly, these and similar Associations may help female migrants with some of their issues and challenges but employees there are not professional lawyers or psychologists.

Centers of psychological and legal support for migrants

There are some organizations in Turkey that exist to end all types of violence and abuse against women and girls and domestic and sexual violence. These can help female migrants from the countries of the Former Soviet Union in difficult situations of their lives. One of the organizations is Mor Catı Women's Shelter Foundation. The Mor Catı Women's Shelter Foundation (in Turkish: Mor Catı Kadın Sıgınagı Vakfı) functions effectively and protects women from violence and abuse. [43]

A Centre of psychological and legal support to migrants should be created in Istanbul, which could be sponsored by one of the universities. I took the idea of this centre from a Working Group of the Department of Psychiatry and Psychotherapy of the German university hospital "Charite" [44] in Berlin, where the Working Group for Intercultural Research on Migration and the Health Sector is situated. This working group helps migrants who are passing through the difficult stages of immigrants' life in a host country. As noted these stages have been called 'Cultural Shock'.

This working group is interdisciplinary, multi-professional and intercultural, consisting of professionals from the fields of psychiatry, psychology, psychotherapy, social work and nursing. The academic framework enables research projects as well as treatment and guidance services, thus offering the opportunity to carry out research as well as to teach and to heal.

I would like to propose creating a Center of psychological and legal support for migrants, sponsored by one of the universities in Istanbul that can really help female migrants from the countries of the Former Soviet Union, who are in Turkey on a voluntary basis. The volunteers would be students and these student-volunteers would help the female migrants in the area of Turkish Law and offer psychological support. It would be

---

[43] Mor Catı Women's Shelter Foundation (Mor Catı Kadın Sıgınagı Vakfı). Accessed 1 June 2016. https://www.morcati.org.tr/en/.

[44] The Charite. Department of Psychiatry and Psychotherapy. Working Group for Intercultural Research on Migration and the Health Sector. Accessed 1 June 2016. https://psy-ccm.charite.de/en/research/ cross_cultural_research _on_ migration _and_ mental_health _care_social_psychiatry /working_group_for_ intercultural_ research _on_migration_and_the_health_sector/.

good practice for the students, especially for future lawyers and psychologists, and for female migrants it would provide very important professional help with their issues.

The Center would not incur any additional expense because students would help female migrants through the Internet and social networks. For the student-volunteers it would be very good practice in their future professions and they could accumulate professional experience and good material for their future diplomas. For female migrants it would be help in the solving of their issues in the host country.

In my opinion, adopting a positive international experience is essential to the development of any society and if such a Center were operating in Istanbul it would be a real benefit to both students-volunteers and female migrants alike.

I conclude that female migrants in any difficult situation in their lives may receive help in Turkey from some state and non-governmental institutions: from the Turkish police; from Embassies and Consulates of their own countries of origin; from associations of compatriots, from the Mor Catı Women's Shelter Foundation and the Center of psychological and legal support to migrants.

The Center of psychological and legal support to migrants should be created by one of the universities in Istanbul and could really help female migrants from the countries of the Former Soviet Union in Turkey, using student-volunteers.

Conclusions

Female migration is a common phenomenon in the contemporary world and a lot of women try to find a better standard of life abroad via marriage because in their mind this is the easiest way to live abroad.

Female migration to Turkey can arise through poverty, unemployment, low standard of living, or lack of prospects in the countries of the Former Soviet Union.

There is a pattern that the greatest flows of migrants come from the poorest countries of the Former Soviet Union. Thus, according to the results of my research, fewer migrants to Turkey were from the three Baltic countries, which are the most successful countries among the countries of the Former USSR. The biggest flows of female migrants were from the countries of Central Asia, Ukraine and Russia.

The majority of women think that they can solve all their material and financial problems by migration and marriage to foreigners. However, the reality that we found when carrying out the research about the migration of women was different. We found discrimination, violence, lack of understanding and respect, language barriers, lack of opportunities to work and build a career - in fact women face many problems abroad.

The majority of women from the countries of the Former Soviet Union, who would like to stay permanently in the host country, need to start learning how to survive in a different culture, with different traditions and a different religion in Turkey. This is because international married couples are two very different people who have come together and if they have no common language they are unable to discuss their different views on their future life.

The majority of Turkish men see their wives in the kitchen and with their children, whereas a lot of women would like to fulfil themselves as professionals building their career in the host country. Conflict in the family is very likely to arise from this.

Women, who come to Turkey from different countries of the Former Soviet Union, have similar problems in the host country. The majority of them have difficulties in learning the Turkish language and adapting to the culture and traditions. For some of them this process of adaptation may take years, some will never find their own place in the host country and will return to their country of origin.

Women, who would like to stay in their professions in the host country, need to travel a long and a difficult road. Firstly, they must have the consent of their husbands to work, because, as noted, the majority of men do not want to see their wives employed. Secondly, they need to study the language of their new country and to learn it very well. Thirdly, they need to go through the complicated procedure of gaining recognition of their academic diplomas in Turkey. This procedure may take years and few women achieve it.

The women need help and support in the host country. They can find some information and support themselves in the Embassies and Consulates of their own countries, but, in my opinion, it would be wonderful to open a Center of psychological and legal support for migrants in one of universities in Istanbul. This could be a really important in giving psychological and legal support to migrants in Turkey.

The research covered women from the countries of the Former Soviet Union who are married in Turkey, who stay permanently and legally in the country, who have children and who are 'visible' women in general.

Another group of 'visible' women, who participated in the research, were female labor migrants from the countries of the Former Soviet Union, often working illegally. The percentage of these women in the research was much smaller than the women who came to the country seeking marriage. These female migrants keep in contact in their groups of the same labor migrants and they do not want contact with outside groups. Contacting them was problematic.

However, in Turkey are also women from the countries of the Former USSR who work there, but who are 'invisible'. Who knows why and how they first appeared in Turkey but it is fact that some women from the Former USSR work in Turkey as prostitutes. They could not be a part of this research for several reasons but these women do exist in the country. Maybe sometime in the future they will be the subject of other scientific research in Turkey.

Children of women from the countries of the Former Soviet Union were not subjects of this research but it is necessary to note that the majority of the women have children: 60% of women from Armenia; 100% of women from Azerbaijan; 80% of women from Belarus; 78% of women from Georgia; 62% from Kazakhstan; 63% from Kyrgyzstan; 17% from Latvia; 85% from Moldova; 70% from Russia; 50% from Tajikistan; 91% from Turkmenistan; 69% from Ukraine; and 86% from Uzbekistan.

In general, 70% of women who participated in this research have children from previous or current marriages in Turkey. Some of the children of these women have remained in their mother's country of origin, some have come with their mothers to Turkey and are remaining permanently; others were born in Turkey. The detailed characteristics of the children of these women, the analysis of their age and gender and the results of this analysis will form a chapter of a further book or another article.

This book offers some preliminary insights into the lives and experiences of female movers from the countries of former Soviet Union when they move to Turkey. There are also some basic characteristics about their motives for migration which are presented as part of the wider context where Turkey's economic and political circumstances are briefly contrasted with the profiles of those of the sending countries. There are significant differences between these countries of origin and Turkey, as well as such differences among themselves. Thus, it is no suprrise that a sizeable volume of females moved from these countries to Turkey. Referring to pull factors, along with economic indicators, a demographic measure has also been considered as the male share in Turkey's population was larger than females leading to a demand for female immigrants.

There is obvious need for more studies and analyses in each and every one of these topical areas. Hence this book was aimed at offering a broad understanding of the female movers from these countries in Turkey and highlighting the key areas of concern which may be picked up by researchers and policy makers in the future.

REFERENCES

Agadjanian, L. and V. Agadjanian. 2010. "Marriage, childbearing, and migration in Kyrgyzstan: Exploring interdependencies." *Demographic Research*, 22(7), pp. 159-188.

Ashman, A.M. and Gokmen, J. E. (2006). *Tales from the Expat Harem: Foreign Women in Modern Turkey* (Seal Women's Travel). Berkeley, CA: Seal Press.

Becker, G. S. 1993. *Human Capital: A Theoretical and Empirical Analysis, with Special Reference to Education, 3d edition.* Chicago: The University of Chicago Press.

Burke, J., 2014. "Post-Soviet world: what you need to know about the 15 states." *The Guardian.* Accessed 20 May 2016. https://www.theguardian.com/world/2014/jun/09/-sp-profiles-post-soviet-states.

Cohen, J. H. and I. Sirkeci. 2011. *Cultures of Migration, the Global Nature of Contemporary Mobility.* University of Texas Press, Austin, USA.

Encyclopedia Britannica. 2016. "Turkic languages." Accessed 26 May 2016. http://www.britannica.com/topic/Turkic-languages.

Eurostat. Accessed March, 2016. http://ec.europa.eu/eurostat/ tgm/ table.do?tab=table&init=1&language=en&pcode=tps00155&plug in=1.

Expat Guide Turkey. 2013. "New Law on Foreigners and International Protection." Accessed 15 May 2016. https://www.expatguideturkey. com/new-law-on-foreigners-and-international-protection/.

Focus Economics. 2016. Economic Indicators, News and Forecasts. Accessed May 1. http://www.focus-economics.com/ countries/ turkey.

Grigonis, R., 2014. "Images of the 12 Most Popular World Religions and Sects." *Newsmax Media.* Accessed 3 May 2016. http://www.newsmax.com/TheWire/most-popular-religions-sects-images/2014/05/01/id/569022/.

Gulcin, G. P., E. Ballı, and M. Tekeoglu. 2014. "Purchasing Power Parity in Commonwealth of Independent States." *International conference on Eurasian Economies*, pp. 1-5.

Guveli, A. Ganzeboom, H., Baykara-Krumme, H., Platt, L., Eroglu, S., Barakdar, S., Nauck, B., Sozeri, E.K. and Spierings, N. (2015). *Intergenerational consequences of migration: socio-economic, family and cultural patterns of stability and change in Turkey and Europe.* Palgrave Macmillan, Houndmills, Basingstoke.

Hewitt, G., 2015. *The Abkhazians: A Handbook (Caucasus World: Peoples of the Caucasus).* Routledge.

Heyat, F., 2002. *Azeri Women in Transition: Women in Soviet and Post-Soviet Azerbaijan*. London and New York: Routledge.

Huberta, von Voss (ed.). 2007. *Portraits of Hope. Armenians in the Contemporary World*. New York and Oxford: Berghahn Books.

Ieconomics. 2016. "Search & Visualization of Economic Indicators." Accessed May 1. http://ieconomics.com/.

Index Mundi. 2015. http://www.indexmundi.com/. Accessed 15 May 2016.

International Labor Organization (ILO). 1995. Turkey - Constitutional law - Constitution - Act No.4121 of 23 July 1995 amending the preamble and certain articles of Act No.2709 of 7 November 1982 concerning the Constitution of the Republic of Turkey. Adoption: 1995-07-23. Date of entry into force: 1995-07-26. TUR-1995-C-42905. Accessed 10 May 2016. http://www.ilo.org/dyn/natlex/natlex4.listResults? p_lang=en&p_country=TUR&p_classification=01.01.

ILO. 1998. "Agreement between Turkey and Georgia on Social Security." Signed at Izmir on 11 December 1998. Resmi Gazete, 2003-11-12, No.25287, pp. 57-69. Accessed 10 May 2016. http://www.ilo.org/dyn/ natlex/natlex4.detail? p_lang=en&p_isn =65891&p_country   =TUR&p_count=781&p_classification =23.01 &p_classcount=71.

ILO. 1998. "Agreement between the Government of the Republic of Turkey and the Government of Azerbaijan on Social Security. Signed at Ankara on 17 July 1998. Resmi Gazete, 2001-01-22, No.24295, pp. 284-309. Accessed 10 May 2016. http://www.ilo.org/dyn/natlex/   natlex4.detail?p_lang=en&p_ isn=61727&p_country=TUR&p_   count=781&p_classification= 23.01&p_classcount=71.

ILO. 2009. "The Turkish Citizenship Law." Act No. 5901. Official Gazette, 2009-06-12, No.27256. Accessed 5 May 2016. http://www.ilo.org/ dyn/natlex/natlex4.detail? p_lang=en&p_isn= 85849&p_country= TUR&p_count=781.

Investopedia. 2016. "Human Capital." Accessed 8 May 2016. http://www.investopedia.com/terms/h/humancapital.asp.

Investopedia. 2016. "Per Capita GDP." Accessed May 2. http://www.investopedia.com/terms/p/per-capita-gdp.asp.

Investopedia. 2016. "Purchasing Power Parity - PPP." Accessed 7 May 2016. http://www.investopedia.com/terms/p/ppp.asp.

Investopedia. 2016. "What causes human capital to depreciate?" Accessed 28 May 2016. http://www.investopedia.com/ask/ answers/021615/what-causes-human-capital-depreciate.asp.

Irwin. R., 2007. "Culture shock: negotiating feelings in the field." *Anthropology Matters*. 9(1). Accessed 2/6/2016. http://www.

anthropologymatters.com/index.php/anth_matters/article/view/64/ 123.

Jovanovic, M. N. 2007. *The Economics of International Integration.* Edward Elgar Publishing.

Koshulko, O., and G. Onkal. 2015. "Issues in countries of the former Soviet Union as the driving force for female migration to Turkey." *International Letters of Social and Humanistic Sciences*, 56, pp. 120-126. doi:10.18052/www.scipress. com/ILSHS.56.120.

Koshulko, O., and V. Koshulko. 2012. *Human capital in Ukraine: how we do not value what we have.* Lap Lambert Academic Publishing, Germany.

Koshulko. O., 2008. "Human Capital Management in the Retail Food Industry." Manuscript. The dissertation on gaining the Economic Sciences Candidate degree on the speciality 08.00.04 - economics and management of enterprises. National University of Food Technologies, Kyiv. Accessed 25 May 2016. http://enuftir.nuft.edu.ua/jspui/ handle/123456789/13660.

Koshulko. O., 2015. "Exploring of the Human Capital Depreciation of Ukrainian Labor Migrants Abroad: Results of a Survey." *International Letters of Social and Humanistic Sciences*, 64, pp. 66-72, doi: 10.18052/www.scipress.com/ILSHS.64.66.

Koshulko. O., 2016. "Discourse about Women-Immigrants from Former Soviet Union Countries as a Special Social Group in Turkey." In: *Gender in Transnational Societies: Feminist Scholarship and Personal Narratives* edited by Rujuta Chincholkar-Mandelia and Moiyattu Banya, pp. 165-167, Cognella Academic Publishing, San Diego, USA.

Laruelle, M., 2013. *Kazakhstan: Central Asia's New Migration Crossroads.* Brill Publishing House. pp. 87-108.

Mor Catı Women's Shelter Foundation (Mor Catı Kadın Sığınagı Vakfı). Accessed 1 June 2016. https://www.morcati.org.tr/en/.

Nafziger, J. A. R., R. K. Paterson, and A. D. Renteln. 2014. *Cultural Law - International, Comparative, and Indigenous.* Cambridge University Press.

Oberg, K., 1960. "Culture Shock: Adjustment to New Cultural Environments." *Practical Anthropology*, 7, pp. 177-182.

Ozgur, E.M, A. Deniz, D. Hasta, M.M. Yucesahin, & S. Yavuz. 2014. "The Immigration of Russians and Azerbaijanis to Antalya (Turkey): Who are They? Why Are They Here?" *Insight Turkey*, Ankara, Turkey, 16(4), pp. 105-123.

Ozmore, S., 2013. "The Sultanate of Women." Saints, Sisters, and Sluts. Accessed 1 May 2016. http://saintssistersandsluts. com/the-sultanate-of-women/.

Parliament of Turkey. 2012. "The Law to Protect Family and Prevent Violence Against Women." Law No.6284 from 8 March 2012.

Accessed 8 June 2016. http://www.lawsturkey.com/law/law-to-protect-family-and-prevent-violence-against-woman-6284.

Parliament of Turkey. 2013. Law No.6458 on Foreigners and International Protection, 4 April 2013. Accessed May 8. http://www.refworld.org/docid/5167fbb20.html.

Pelkmans, M., 2006. *Defending the border: identity, religion, and modernity in the Republic of Georgia*. Ithaca, New York: Cornell University Press.

Piper, N., and A. French. 2011. "Do Women Benefit from Migration? An Editorial Introduction." Special issue "Female Migration Outcomes: Human Rights Perspectives." *Diversities*. 13(1), pp. 1-3. Accessed 20 June 2016. http://www.mmg. mpg.de/subsites/diversities/past-issues/female-migration-outcomes/editorial-introduction-do-women-benefit-from-migration/.

Quran. Surah Al-Baqarah [2:183-185]. Accessed 8 May 2016. http://quran.com/2/183-185.

Quran. Surah Al-Baqarah [2:221]. Accessed 8 May 2016. http://quran.com/2/221.

Saunders, B., 2015. *Overeducated and Over Here: Skilled EU Migrants in Britain*. London: Transnational Press London, 140 pages.

Sawma, G., 2013. "Muslim Men Marrying Non-Muslim Women." *International Law*. Accessed 5 May 2016. http://gabrielsawma. blogspot.com/2013/07/muslim-men-marrying-non-muslim-women_5.html.

Sevinclidir, P., 2015. "Beyond the headscarf: Turkey's women struggle for equality." *The BBC News*. Accessed 5 June 2016. http://www.bbc.com/news/world-europe-32982780.

Sirkeci, I., 2009. "Transnational mobility and conflict." *Migration Letters*, 6(1). pp. 3-14.

Sirkeci, I., and J. H. Cohen. 2016. "Cultures of migration and conflict in contemporary human mobility in Turkey." *European Review*, 24(3), pp. 381-396.

Sirkeci, I., N. Acik, and B. Saunders. 2014. "Discriminatory labour market experiences of A8 national high skilled workers in the UK." *Border Crossing*, 4(1-2). pp. 17-31.

Sookhdeo, R., 2007. *Why Christian Women Convert to Islam*. Isaac Publishing, USA.

Sorokin, P., 1998. *Social mobility*. London: Routledge / Thoemmes.

Suad, J., and A. Nagmabadi. 2003. *Encyclopedia of Women and Islamic Cultures: Family, Law and Politics*. Leiden: Brill.

Sumer, A. U. and Boray, I. (2013). *Ataturk's Reforms Empowered Turkish Women and Set Example for the Developing World: A look at the remarkable transformation of a Nation*. Ataturk

Society of America, Washington, USA. Accessed 8 May 2016. http://www.light millennium.org/ataturk/2013/asa-paper2.pdf.

The Charite. Department of Psychiatry and Psychotherapy. Working Group for Intercultural Research on Migration and the Health Sector. Accessed 1 June 2016. https://psy-ccm.charite .de/en/research/ cross_cultural_research_on_ migration_and_ mental_health_care_social_psychiatry/working_group_for_interc ultural_research_on_migration_and_the_health_sector/.

The Christian Broadcasting Network. 2016. "Why Christian Women Marry Muslim Men." Accessed 3 May 2016. http://www1.cbn .com/ marriage/why-christian-women-marry-muslim-men.

The Conference Board of Canada. 2016. "Income Per Capita." Accessed May 3. http://www.conferenceboard.ca/hcp/details/ economy/income-per-capita.aspx.

The Economic Times: Business News, Personal Finance, Financial News. 2016. "Definition of 'Purchasing Power Parity'." Accessed 12 May 2016. http://economictimes.indiatimes.com/definition/ purchasing-power-parity.

The Economic Times: Business News, Personal Finance, Financial News. 2016. "Human Development Index." Accessed 13 May 2016. http://economictimes.indiatimes.com/definition/human-development-index.

The Law of Turkey. 2001. "The Law on Individual Pension Savings and Investment System No.4632" (Date of Ratification 28 March 2001; Date of Publication 7 April 2001). Accessed 8 June 2016. http://www.sigortadenetim.org/mevzuat/ngilizce-mevzuat/118.html.

The Law of Turkey. 2006. "Turkish Social Security and Universal Health Insurance Law: 5510" (The date of enactment of the Law was 31 May 2006, and the date of entry into force was 01 October 2008). Accessed 8 June 2016. http://turkishlaborlaw.com/turkish-social-security-law-no-5510.

The Ministry of Foreign Affairs of the Republic of Turkey (2016) http://www.mfa.gov.tr/. Accessed 1 June 2016.

The United States Department of State (DOS). 2016. "Dual Nationality." Accessed 15 May 2016. https://travel.state.gov/ content/travel/en/legal-considerations/us-citizenship-laws-policies/citizenship-and-dual-nationality/dual-nationality.html.

The University of Chicago Press. Gary S. Becker. Human Capital: A Theoretical and Empirical Analysis, with Special Reference to Education, 3d edition. Accessed 18 May 2016. http:// press .uchicago .edu/ucp/books/book/chicago/H/bo3684031.html.

The World Bank. 2016. "GDP per capita, PPP (current international $)." Accessed 13 May 2016. http://data.worldbank.org/indicator /NY.GDP.PCAP.PP.CD.

Theodore, W. Schultz. 1961. "Investment in Human Capital." *The American Economic Review*. 51(1), pp. 1-17.

Trading Economics. Accessed March, 2016. http://www.trading economics.com/armenia/wages.

Transparency International. 2015. "Corruption perception index 2015." Accessed 20 May 2016. https://www.transparency.org/cpi2015/.

Turkish Statistical Institute. 2016. "Population by years, age group and sex, 1935-2015." Accessed 20 April 2016. http://www.turkstat.gov.tr/UstMenu.do?metod=kategorist.

TV Channel 1+1. 2012. The program "Change a woman." Accessed 17 May 2016. https://www.youtube.com/watch?v=eteiA0t84YA.

Unal, Bayram. 2008. *Ethnic division of labor: The Moldovan migrant women in In-House Services in Istanbul*. PhD Thesis, State University of New York at Binghamton.

UNDP - United Nations Development Programme. 2014. "Human Development Reports." Accessed 13 May 2016. http://hdr.undp.org/en/composite/HDI.

UNHCR - United Nations High Commissioner for Refugees. 2016. "States Parties to the 1951 Convention and its 1967 Protocol." Accessed May 4. http://www.unhcr.org/3b73b0d63.html.

UNHCR. 2015. "2015 UNHCR subregional operations profile - Eastern Europe." Accessed May 10. http://www.unhcr.org/pages/49e48d4d6.html.

World Economic Forum. 2014. "Global Gender Gap Index 2014." Accessed 5 May 2016. http://www3.weforum.org/docs/GGGR14/GGGR_CompleteReport_2014.pdf.

XE. 2016. "The World's Trusted Currency Authority." Accessed March 3. http://www.xe.com/

Zirin, Mary, Irina Livezeanu, Christine D. Worobec and June Pachuta-Farris. 2007. *Women & Gender in Central and Eastern Europe, Russia, And Eurasia: A Comprehensive Bibliography*. Vol. I: Southeastern and East Central Europe, M.E. Sharpe.